T

THE ISLAND SERIES

‡Achill
†The Aran Islands
 Alderney
 The Isle of Arran
 The Island of Bute
*Canary Islands: Fuerteventura
*Cape Breton Island
*Corsica
*‡Cyprus
*Dominica
*The Falkland Islands
*Grand Bahama
†Harris and Lewis
†The Isle of Mull
 Lundy
 The Maltese Islands
†Orkney
*Puerto Rico
 St Kilda and Other Hebridean Islands
*‡The Seychelles
†Shetland
*‡Sicily
*‡Singapore
‡Skye
*‡The Solomon Islands
*Vancouver Island

in preparation
 Bermuda
 Mauritius
 Rhodes
 St Helena
 Tasmania
 Tobago
 The Uists and Barra

* Published in the United States by Stackpole
† Published in the United States by David & Charles
‡ The series is distributed in Australia by Wren

GOTLAND

by *ARTHUR SPENCER*

DAVID & CHARLES

NEWTON ABBOT LONDON NORTH POMFRET (VT) VANCOUVER

ISBN 0 7153 6373 5

Set in 11 on 13 point Baskerville and printed in
Great Britain by Latimer Trend & Company
Ltd Plymouth for David & Charles (Holdings)
Limited South Devon House Newton Abbot
Devon

Published in the United States of America by
David & Charles Inc North Pomfret Vermont
05053 USA

Published in Canada by Douglas David &
Charles Limited 3645 McKechnie Drive
West Vancouver BC

CONTENTS

ILLUSTRATIONS

ILLUSTRATIONS

Photographs not acknowledged above are reproduced by courtesy of the Gotland Tourist Association

MAPS

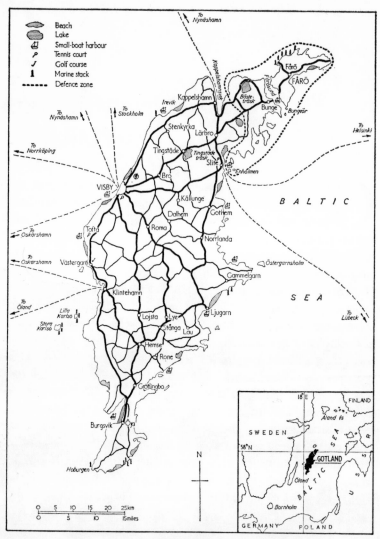

General map

1 POSITION, STRUCTURE AND APPEARANCE

GOTLAND is the biggest island in the Baltic and the most easterly province of Sweden. It lies between latitudes 58° 00' and 56° 55' N and longitudes 18° 18' and 19° 21' E and covers an area of 1,212sq miles (3,140sq km). From its northernmost point (on the island of Fårö, which is normally considered part of Gotland) to its southern tip is 96 miles (155km), while its greatest width is 33 miles (53km). Visby, the capital (57° 39' N, 18° 18' E), is about as far north as Aberdeen, the middle of Hudson's Bay or the Isle of Skye; and as far east as Budapest or Brindisi. From Visby to the nearest point on the Swedish mainland is 55 miles, to the nearest harbour 62. This is Västervik—'West Creek', but west to the Gotlanders, not the Swedes, which sheds an interesting light on early patterns of Baltic trade. The shortest route from Gotland to Sweden is from Klintehamn, two-thirds of the way down the west coast, to Böda on the island of Öland, a leg of only 45 miles with land in sight most of the way and thus a very old 'island-hopping' route. To the east it is 95 miles to the coast of Latvia, to the south 135 miles to the Polish coast near Gdynia.

FIRST IMPRESSIONS

A long low line on the edge of the sea—that is one's first sight of Gotland. Soon the predominant colours can be made out, dark green on grey, where the pine forests top the limestone

11

cliffs. From the air the dappled countryside rushes nearer. Then—suddenly—far below are the toy walls and towers of a fairytale Visby. Its bright pattern of red roofs, black roofs, grey walls, pastel-coloured buildings and green gardens glows like a rare piece of the Baltic amber it has traded in for so long. Like a glittering gem it lies in an oval setting, part moat, part sea.

From the deck of a ship the scene shifts more slowly. The occasional spikes like enormous trees that break the flat mass of the forest resolve themselves into church steeples, the first glimpse of these splendid buildings. The undercut craggy cliffs, the windmills and other prominent features stand out more clearly. The skyline alters as the ship throbs on. Visby looms up behind the long sea wall and glistening harbour across the last stretch of estranging sea—towers, tall houses, grey ribs of ruined churches, roofs and buildings, brick-red, copper-red, black and white, and above all the majestic cathedral. A medieval Manhattan!

More than geography separates Gotland and its people from the rest of Sweden. To enter Visby, whether from the harbour or through some noble gate in the intact landward walls, is to be transported to a different age and a faraway land. The scale, as in the set of a medieval play, is intimate, the backdrop varied. Half-timbered houses lean towards each other across cobbled streets. Mysterious high walls shelter russet-coloured cottages and bright gardens. Pastel-hued arcades hide small shops selling ancient wares—amber, silver and carved wood. Intriguing alleys lead to the great grey houses of the Hansa Merchants, or to the gaunt ruins of a lovely church.

On such a stage as this the Visby burghers go about their business. Proud of their great heritage, of more mixed descent than most Swedes, they, like other Gotlanders, retain the canny individualism of the islander and a strong sense of community. Closer to nature than the softer inhabitants of over-swollen cities, and closer too in a small society to the traditions of their forebears, they are more conservative, both politically and personally, than mainland Swedes. This trait has not, however, prevented them from frequently being the first in the country to take a radical new step: but they have to be convinced of its value. There is no change for the sake of change. They respond to an interest in the unique island of which they are so proud, but, like the Scots or the Spaniards, respect the privacy of others. Visitors are not pestered, but, if they need it, will get any amount of friendly, somewhat self-deprecating, help.

Visby apart, the countryside makes a memorable impact. It is on a small scale but sometimes quite spectacular in a peaceful, satisfying way—dark forests against yellow corn, sheets of colour where flowers luxuriate, shimmering lakes, the broken shade of woodland paths or the green expanse of windy turf above abrupt grey cliffs. Such are the impressions of this lovely island the visitor will retain, together with more thought-provoking memories of the remarkable monuments of vanished ages—great cairns, stone ships and splendid churches.

GOTLAND PROPER

Gotland proper is an undulating limestone plateau from 85 to 140ft high with a few detached hills rising above it and some important belts of sandstone in the south. The highest points (274ft, 83m) are at the quaintly named hamlet of Sion, 4 miles south of Visby and on an undistinguished hump south-east of Klintehamn near Lojsta village. The plateau of Torsburgen (Hill of Thor), 223ft high and situated somewhat east of the centre of the island, and the man-faced bluff of Hoburgen at the southern point are more impressive, from their siting rather than their actual size. Like the islands of Stora Karlsö and Lilla Karlsö off the west coast and other prominent knolls and crags on Gotland they were formed as islands in an ancient sea bigger and deeper than the present Baltic, when the rest of the surrounding land was under water.

Most of the present coast rises abruptly from the sea. This is particularly noticeable when one approaches Visby from sea-ward and thus early presents a true, and a lasting, impression of the island's character. In the east and south-east there are gently sloping beaches with offlying rocks and islets. In fact the whole island tilts gradually from north-west to south-east. The grain of the land, however—limestone ridges with glacial top-soil in the hollows between them—runs from north-east to south-west, as the Geological map on p 20 shows. In this it follows the direction of the primeval bedrock deep below—Cambrian deposits at the bottom, Ordovician above them, then the Silurian which forms the backbone of the landscape we see today. This Silurian limestone was formed over 400 million years ago and is overlaid with marls and gravels in the centre and sandstone in the south-west. The stratum, of which Gotland is a very visible part above the sea, curves in a great arc from north-east to south-west from the coast of Estonia to Poland. Its western edge is only a few miles off Visby, and it is primarily this limestone which gives Gotland its distinctive character and marks it off from the older rocks of different colour and texture on the Swedish mainland opposite. Gotland is also different in that it was unaffected by the great heavings of the earth's crust which formed the mountains of Scandi-navia's backbone, the 'keel' as it is called, between Norway and Sweden.

When these Silurian deposits were laid down, most of the world was under water; and the island's cliffs and rocky out-crops are made up of the petrified skeletons of countless myriads of aquatic animals. The sea, which teemed with them, was warm because the place we now know as Gotland was only about 10 degrees north of the then equator; near relations of creatures whose fossils are found in the island's limestone still live in appropriate conditions in today's tropical seas. Indeed, so many important discoveries from this crucial period in the development of life on our planet have been made on Gotland, whether because it is specially rich in remains or because they are so common and so obvious that they stimulated the interest of pioneer palaeontologists, that, until only a few years ago, the era now uniformly designated Silurian was often known as Gotlandian.

Over 1,500 species of animals from this fecund age have been identified on Gotland to date; and the work has recently been given further encouragement by the establishment of a residential research station at Allekvia, a few miles from Visby. To the layman most of the fossils which so excite the experts seem somewhat dull and are often very small. Yet there is no denying the beauty and fascination of some of them. There are large clumps of intricate coral and curling 'sea-lilies', delicate as frost-flowers on a windowpane. Even the closely packed skeletons of much smaller animals, in themselves of little aesthetic merit, have a beauty of their own when the split stone is polished to bring out their shape. Indeed the polished sections of the distinctive marble from Hoburgen or Stora Karlsö are virtually prepared exhibits of the remains of these fantastically prolific creatures.

It is obvious even to the untutored eye that many of them are snails of a sort. And it is a succession of different snails that has, scientifically speaking, provided some of the most significant material of great importance to the dating of the various strata up to quite recent times. Fossils of other familiar animals abound—mussels, cuttlefish (much more numerous and comprising more different species than now) and others. So do those of well known and widespread forms of marine life now extinct—trilobites, stromatoporoids (whose calcified remains are common enough to have been given the local name of 'cat-skull'), eurypterids (the ancient aquatic relatives of scorpions, which sometimes reached a length of 9ft) and other tongue-twisters best left to the specialists.

There have, however, been several discoveries worth mentioning for their general interest. One of the earliest was for long thought to be epoch-making as representing the first known land animal and, incidentally, as proof of the existence of hitherto unknown outcrops of dry land in the great Silurian Sea. This was a primitive form of scorpion (*palaeophonus*) found in 1885 in the limestone terraces on which Visby stands. Alas! it is now known that these beasts lived in the water. On the other hand, in 1952 the Danish *Galatea* expedition hauled out from 1,800 fathoms under the Pacific a snail closely related to a common Gotlandic fossil (*pilina*) and named it *neopilina* in its honour.

Similar finds are to be expected as knowledge of the oceans increases. So far as Gotland is concerned, however, they are likely to make sense only in relation to the Silurian Age, for after it until quite recent times the island has produced only the smallest clues to what happened to it and on it. Successive ice-caps obliterated evidence of conditions between the Silurian period and the end of the latest Ice Age, about 11,000 years ago, but a fairly detailed account of subsequent events can be given. It is obvious that before this Gotland had moved north as the continents drifted. The land took shape, battered by cata-clysmic storms, ground and gouged by sea and ice. The last Ice Age has left many traces of its power. Great boulders from many miles farther north lie where the melting ice stranded them. The biggest is at Rone in the south-east, the granite *Bastustainen* (the 'Bath-house Stone'), 26ft long, 22ft broad and 16ft high. The great Swedish botanist, Linnaeus (Carl von Linné), was particularly curious about these huge isolated blocks of a stone entirely different from anything else on the island. He correctly deduced that they had come from, among other places, the Åland Islands, over 300 miles to the north, but wrongly assumed that they had been rolled from there by mighty waves.

The ice has also left other visible evidence of its presence. In many places the ground is scored by ice-rills running from north-east to south-west, as, for example, just to the south of

Page 17 Visby: (*above*) Old houses in the shelter of the East Wall; (*below*) where the North Wall runs down to the sea. 'Big Liz' Tower with the dry moat in front; St George's Gate and bridge beyond

Page 18 Visby: (*above*) The still medieval sky-line of Visby from Almedalen, site of the old harbour. The Old Apothecary's Shop is on the left above a stretch of the original wall, the square tower of Holy Trinity Church next to it and the cathedral, half hidden by what is left of St Laurence's Church; (*below*) the seventeenth-century Burmeister House in Visby, the well-preserved home of a rich Hanseatic merchant. The earlier step-gabled house on the right is now a youth hostel

POSITION, STRUCTURE AND APPEARANCE

Visby at Halsjärnet. Other remains are more widespread and more important. The water in Tingstäde Lake is held back by a dam of earth left by a melting glacier. The 'meres', formerly so important to fishing and farming, filled depressions caused by the ice pressing on the ground. The best farmland on the island consists of a heavy marl deposited by the ice.

'The Sinking Island'

Since the end of the Ice Age the level of the sea round Gotland has fluctuated by up to 150ft from the present level. Proof of this can be seen all over the island. The terraces on which Visby stands are, as has been mentioned earlier, the shorelines of ancient, deeper seas and they continue quite spectacularly to north and to south. The 'Old Man of Hoburg' got his face and 'The Maiden' (*Jungfrun*) of Lickershamn in the north-west her suggestive lines through the action of the waves. Banks of sand and pebble now well inland mark earlier beaches. In many places marine stacks—cores of harder rock which resisted the scouring of the tides—stand up like sentries guarding their now vanished shore. Even a superficial examination of these phenomena soon discloses that they are on two main, and several subsidiary, levels. In other words, the land kept rising and falling. It is astounding to read exactly this in the *Gutasaga*, compiled in the thirteenth century. It states that, at the time the first man landed on the island, it 'sank by day and rose by night'.

It has, however, been left to modern science to discover that these shifts in sea-level were accompanied by changes in the salinity of the water. Once again it is a series of snails, living either in fresh or salt water, which provides the evidence. Not surprisingly, in view of the amount of ice that melted, the first of these seas in the Baltic basin was of fresh water—which proves that it was an enclosed sea not joined to the salt Atlantic. After some time it did run into the Atlantic across what is now Central Sweden, and the Baltic lake became salt. The land then

19

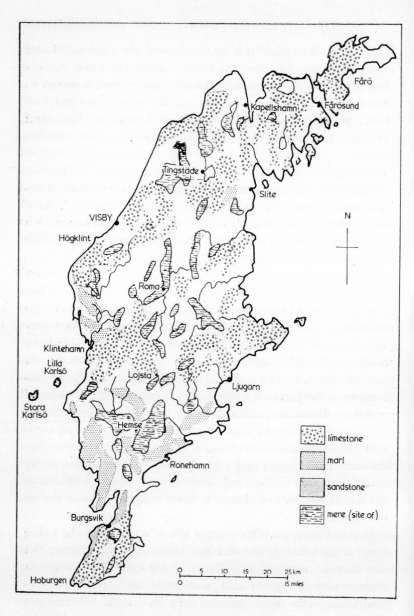

Fårö

Kapellshamn

Fårösund

Tingstäde

Slite

VISBY

Högklint

N

Roma

Klintehamn

Lilla
Karlsö

Lojsta

Ljugarn

Stora
Karlsö

Hemse

	limestone
	marl
	sandstone
	mere (site of)

Ronehamn

Burgsvik

0   5   10   15   20   25 km
0   15 miles

Hoburgen

GEOLOGICAL MAP OF GOTLAND

Geological map

rose again, damming this channel, and the enclosed waters again became fresh; they have been given the name Ancylus Sea from a small pointed freshwater snail (*Ancylus fluviatilis*), first found in strata of this period in 1884 on an 'Ancylus beach' near the big windmills just south of Visby. Its discoverer, Professor Henrik Munthe, a Gotlander and one of the founding fathers of Swedish geological studies, subsequently mapped other beaches of this period with startling results. He showed conclusively that more than half Gotland as we know it was then under water and that the land sloped from north to south more steeply than today; the level of the Ancylus shoreline in the north is about 150ft (45m) above the present level of the sea, and in the south about 63ft (19m).

Since then the levels of land and sea have varied on several occasions. The most important movement was that which caused the land between Denmark and Sweden to sink and the channel we call the Kattegatt to be opened about 8,000 years ago. Through it came the salt sea from the Atlantic so that the Baltic once more became salt; and once more snails (in this case of the salt water *litorina* species), have left their limy remains in perpetual witness of the change. Hence this period is technically known as the Litorina Age, and the new sea the Litorina Sea. This sea was not only about twice as salt as the Baltic now, but also many feet deeper—some 72ft above today's shoreline in the north and 43ft in the south. During this period man first settled on Gotland: and the remains of his habitation are found well inland from the present shore because the sea was higher.

Gotland must then have been wetter and lusher than now, apart from being rather smaller. There is good evidence that the climate was milder. There would still have been the characteristic limestone cliffs and crags, dark green pine trees contrasting with them. Against them in vertical contrast now rise the noble steeples of the many churches—so many that there is hardly a view that does not include at least one. The seasons add their own distinctive vivid colours (or the glistening white of winter's snow).

Flowers and crops are discussed in detail later in this book, but it is appropriate to mention here the visual qualities of some of the commoner, for they have a marked effect on the island's appearance, and on the visitor's memories. The brilliant blue of chicory or viper's bugloss against golden corn with a framework of bold pink willowherb (fireweed) setting off the almost black conifers—these are typical of high summer. Early summer evokes green turf on a humpy headland, with the limestone ribs and boulders smothered with pink or yellow orchids. Elsewhere there are the glistening 'meres' dappled with waterlilies and bordered by highly ornamental reeds. In spite of its comparatively small size and lack of awesome features like high mountains or roaring waterfalls, Gotland has a great variety and often subtle charm. Only in the larger woods—and there are few tracts of solid forest on Gotland—is there any impression of monotony. Normally at a single glance one can conveniently see numerous, but gentle, contrasts of form and colour. It is indeed a beautiful and distinctive place.

NEIGHBOURING ISLANDS

Fårö

Just to the north of Gotland proper, and separated from it by the elliptical waters of Fårösund, lies Fårö (Sheep Island), a crescent-shaped island of about 43sq miles (112sq km), curving from north-east to south-west. In a straight line it is 12½ miles (19km) long and 5 miles (8km) across at its widest point. The coast is deeply indented, and has some of the best examples of marine stacks on the whole of Gotland on the west coast between Digerhuvud and Lauterhorn. The north-east corner has extensive sandhills. The island generally is flat, with a few hillocks in the east and a chain of small lakes in the middle. It is well wooded. Fårösund is an excellent anchorage, which was used by the British Fleet occasionally in the Napoleonic Wars and by a combined squadron of British and French ships for two successive years in the Crimean War (1853 and 1854) as a base for blockading Russia (see p 80). At the time of writing the famous Swedish film producer Ingmar Bergman has a house on Fårö. The island was formerly an important centre for seal-fishing and trapping seabirds. The whole island is within the Gotland Defence Zone and may therefore be visited by foreigners only on conducted tours or with special permission.

Lilla Karlsö and Stora Karlsö

Lilla Karlsö (Little Charles Island) and Stora Karlsö (Big Charles Island) lie $1\frac{1}{2}$ and $3\frac{1}{2}$ miles respectively off the west

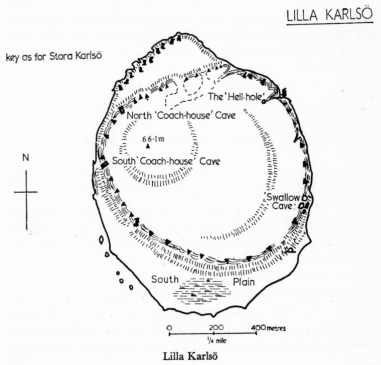

Lilla Karlsö

coast of Gotland about two-thirds of the way down the island. Lilla Karlsö is an oval limestone islet some 1,500 by 1,100yd, 216ft (66m) at its highest point, with precipitous and often undercut sides. There is a spectacular group of marine stacks on its northern point (of which a good view is usually obtained from the boat to Stora Karlsö, which passes close by). On the north-west face of the cliff there is a prominent gully known as the 'Hell Hole', which is the subject of various legends and is mentioned in *Nils Holgersson's Wonderful Journey* by Selma Lagerlöf. There are remains of early inhabitants, probably from about 500 BC, but the island is now uninhabited.

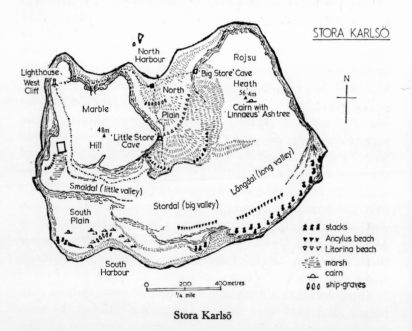

Stora Karlsö

Stora Karlsö is roughly rectangular in shape and about twice the size of its sister island (just under 1sq mile, or 235 hectares), but it is not as high (184ft, 56m). The high ground forms a crescent, with horns to the north encircling a valley which slopes down gently to the shore from the base of a bluff following the line of the high ground. In the middle of the shore is a landing-place grandiloquently entitled 'North Harbour' (Norderhamn) to distinguish it from a similar, but smaller, strip of approachable beach on the southern shore of the island known as 'South Harbour' (Suderhamn). The northern beach is the only one now in regular use, and it is here that the tourist excursions from Klintehamn land. Apart from the valley behind North Harbour (which is known as 'North Plain') and the flat low peninsula near South Harbour ('South Plain'), the island's coast is sheer and unapproachable, with a short steep foreshore along much of it. On the south-east is a long line of marine stacks, and on the north-west the abrupt headland of Västerberget, with the largest concentration of seabirds in Sweden. In particular thousands of guillemots, found in much smaller numbers in only two other places in the Baltic (Bornholm and Bonden, well to the north) breed here.

The rim of North Plain marks the shoreline of the old Ancylus Sea in a quite spectacular fashion (see map, p 24). In the biggest cave then scored out (known as Stora Förvar, the 'Big Store') the first important dig in Sweden (1887) found some of the earliest remains of man in the whole of Scandinavia; they belonged to the Late Stone Age, and above them were deposits from the Bronze and Iron ages and from quite recent times as well, since fishermen and quarrymen working the marble on Marmorberget (Marble Hill) across the valley sought shelter there. Early man also left traces of his activities on South Plain, where there are cairns and ship-graves.

There are other unusual birds besides the guillemots on both islands, and some rare flowers and plants. One of the most curious items in the flora of Stora Karlsö is a stunted ash tree on the bare high ground to the north-east. This is called 'Linnaeus' Ash' and is said to be the tree he described in this place in 1741, since when it has hardly grown at all. The richness and occasional rarity of the plant and bird life on Stora

Karlsö led to it being declared a nature reserve as early as 1880, since when no sheep have been allowed to graze the island. Nor are there now any permanent inhabitants apart from the keepers of the important lighthouse on Västerberget. The islands have for long been in private ownership and may be visited only on conducted tours in the summer or by special permission obtained in Visby.

In appearance both islands stand out boldly from the sea as bumpy slabs of limestone with light grey walls, projecting at the top in many places. Nearer to, considerable variety can be discerned. In particular the groups of marine stacks on the foreshore at several points on both islands look like giant petrified bathers testing the water; it is odd to see how many of these stone columns appear to have heads. North Plain on Stora Karlsö is lush in places, with bright green turf. So are one or two other damp places on the island, especially the swampy pond on the western slope of Marmorberget. Here too there are numerous bushes and small trees, while the path from North Harbour to the lighthouse as it hugs the ancient shoreline, now nearly 100ft above the sea, runs through a comparatively luxuriant copse.

Götska Sandön

Götska Sandön (Sand Island of the Goths) is the fourth of Gotland's neighbour isles. It lies about 25 miles (40km) north of Fårö and is a triangular wooded island just under 10sq miles (26sq km) in area with a maximum height of 138ft (42m). The coast, as might be deduced from its name, has big sand-dunes. The island has remains of Viking and later settlements from the great days of seal-hunting in the Baltic, but only the keepers of the lighthouse on its northern point and their families now live there. The whole island is a national park and protected nature reserve. Like the other islands described above it may be visited only on short conducted tours or by special permission. It is also in the Gotland Defence Zone.

2   CLIMATE, FLORA AND FAUNA

THE climate of Gotland is somewhat better than that of the Swedish mainland opposite. It is a little milder, more equable and usually has much more sun, especially in early summer. But this does not mean that by landing there one steps on to some island in the Caribbean or the Mediterranean. It is still very much in Northern Europe. The climate in fact is intermediate between the unsettled, relatively mild 'Atlantic' weather of the British Isles and the more extreme 'Continental' climate of Russia. To the Swedes Gotland is known for its mild weather and, in local terms, this is justified. Although this is not particularly apparent from meteorological tables, which reduce everything to means and averages, Gotland is significantly milder than eastern Sweden across the water. Roses are sometimes in bloom on Gotland at Christmas. Visby Harbour is icebound only about one winter in ten, the least affected of all Swedish Baltic ports. Some flowers that grow in Gotland are not found again until one travels hundreds of miles farther south.

Being an island, Gotland is breezy: on average there is at least one day each month when winds of gale force (30–40 knots) are recorded at Visby. The prevailing winds are from the south-west the whole year. In winter, as one would expect, they are more frequent; and there is more wind from the south —which keeps back the Arctic cold. Being an island also means that the weather is strongly influenced by the surrounding water, slower than the land both to heat and to cool and thus limiting fluctuations in temperature. The configuration of the

27

neighbouring land whence the prevailing winds come, together with the fact that Gotland stands up as a windbreak, causes depressions to pass either to north or south. These factors also produce fog, especially in the south of the island where sea currents meet, and particularly in April and late summer.

Summer and early autumn tend to be unusually sunny for the latitude. Indeed Gotland holds the record for hours of sunshine for south Sweden from April to September (which justifies the use for the last few years on mail from Visby of a cancellation with the slogan 'The Sun shines more on the Gotland tourist'). June is normally a good month, with some 350hr of sun. So is September. In an average year the temperature in Visby gets up to 27° C (81° F). The sea starts to warm up in June, when the mean surface temperature is 11° C (52° F), and gets to over 13° C (56° F) in September—not comparable with the Bahamas or Malta, but pleasant enough for a quick dip.

The average annual rainfall at Visby is 522mm (20·5in), considerably less than in surrounding countries, except for the south-east tip of Sweden. The wettest times of the year are autumn and January. Spring and early summer are comparatively dry, as the table (p 29) shows. Indeed, partly for this reason and partly because the water-table has been lowered by the draining of previously waterlogged 'meres', drought not infrequently afflicts the farmers at this season. There are no marked variations in relative humidity, which fluctuates between about 75 and 85 per cent. Visby, incidentally, tends to be cloudier early in the day.

The information summarised above has been collected in the last four decades. However, by various methods, such as the analysis of pollen and other plant remains from cores taken from suitable ground, it is possible to get a good idea of how the climate of Gotland has varied since the end of the Ice Age. This historical digression is relevant here since these changes, which are, of course, related to the movements of land and sea described in the previous chapter, have been a major factor in

WEATHER AT VISBY

Lat 57° 39′ N, Long 18° 18′ E
Height above Mean Sea Level, 36ft (11m)
Table compiled from 15 to 48 years' observations, 1901–55

Month	Pressure at MSL Mean	Air Temperature				Relative Humidity		Mean Cloud Amount		Precipitation	
		Mean daily max	Mean daily min	Mean highest in each month	Mean lowest in each month	‖0800	‖1400	‖0800	‖1400	Average Fall	No of days with 1mm or more
	mb	°C	°C	°C	°C	%	%	OKTAS		mm	
January	1013	1	−3	6	−9	86	84	7	7	49	11
February	1013	1	−3	5	−10	84	81	7	6	37	8
March	1013	3	−2	9	−8	83	77	6	5	29	7
April	1013	8	1	15	−4	79	71	5	5	31	6
May	1015	13	5	21	1	74	67	4	4	30	6
June	1013	18	10	25	5	75	68	4	4	33	6
July	1011	21	14	27	10	78	71	4	4	52	7
August	1012	20	13	23	9	73	72	5	4	56	8
September	1014	16	10	21	5	85	75	5	5	50	9
October	1015	11	6	15	1	85	77	6	6	55	11
November	1011	6	3	10	−1	86	83	7	7	52	11
December	1012	3	0	7	−6	86	85	7	7	49	11
Means	1013	10	5	28*	−12†	81	76	6	5	—	—
Totals	—	—	—	—	—	—	—	—	—	522	101
Extreme values	—	—	—	32‡	−25§	—	—	—	—	—	—
No of years' observations	48	30				30		30		30	

* Mean of highest each year
† Mean of lowest each year
‡ Highest recorded temperature
§ Lowest recorded temperature
‖ 0700 and 1300, 1947–55.

Based, with permission of Her Majesty's Stationery Office, on the table in the *Baltic Pilot*, vol II, ninth ed (1965), 88 determining what plants grow on the island now. During the Ancylus period immediately after the ice had gone, the climate was cold and dry. Then various plants whose present habitat is normally the Arctic regions took root on Gotland, as did the pine tree. In the ensuing Litorina Age the climate was much warmer and wetter, and deciduous trees moved in—oaks, elms and limes. About 500 BC the climate again changed for the worse—a harsh and icy age for all the North, which appears to have passed into legend as the dread 'Fimbul Winter' of the old Norse sagas. About the beginning of the Christian era the climate improved again, building up to a peak of warmth with the Little Climatic Optimum of the eleventh and twelfth centuries. This in turn (as the Viking settlers in Vinland learnt to their cost) was followed by what the experts now call the Little Ice Age, which ended with the nineteenth century. All these changes have left their mark on Gotland.

FLORA

Flowers

The brightness and luxuriance of the wildflowers on Gotland in their seasons are as memorable as the presence of species either very rare, or even found nowhere else, in Northern Europe. Whether it is their reaction to the almost perpetual daylight after the long dark winters, or something in the quality of the light—or both—is uncertain, but there is no doubt that many common flowers attain an unusual brilliance and size on Gotland. Possibly it is the complex contrasts of both shape and colour in an essentially small-scale landscape which sets them off to best advantage. Compared with the British Isles at any rate there is also much less spraying of weeds on roadsides, so that wildflowers flourish there. Drainage, new methods of farming, forestry, and the spread of building have in their various ways also affected the plant life of the island in the last 100 years or so.

The earliest account of Gotland's flora was given by two

Danish botanists in the early seventeenth century, and it is clear that it was then richer and more varied than now. A hundred years later a herbarium of plants on Gotland was made and is still extant. In 1741 Linnaeus visited the island, and in his *Gotland Journey* has left valuable observations that confirm and amplify the picture of the classic Gotland landscape. Above all there was much more water about, and in it (as in places it still does) grew sedge (*Cladium mariscus*), much used for litter and thatching houses, and other useful rushes. Cultivated land existed in small plots. The *äng*, a grassy clearing in an open wood, still played its important and traditional role of providing hay—and a habitat for many flowers now scarce, or vanished.

Then, as now, there were to be found some species which were among the first plants to grow on the island after the Ice Age. Both their normal habitat today and their distribution outside it—in Eire, in parts of the Alps and on the Scottish mountains—point to this. A species of asphodel (*Tofieldia calyculata*), mountain avens (*Dryas octopetala*), alpine bartsia (*Bartsia alpina*) and alpine butterwort (*Pinguicula alpina*) are examples of such plants.

The above-mentioned asphodel is not found anywhere else in Northern Europe, and nor are three other monocotyledons— the broad helleborine (*Cephalanthera damasonium*), which in England, where its white and orange-yellow flowers have earned the nickname of 'Poached Egg Plant', is locally common in beechwoods; Spitzel's alpine orchid (*Orchis Spitzeli*), the next habitat of which is 600 miles to the south in Austria; and the purple fen orchid (*Orchis palustris*), which was first found on Gotland in 1799. There are in all thirty-four species of orchid on Gotland and most are protected. In this category, in addition to those mentioned above, are the lady's slipper (*Cypripedium calceolus*), the scented orchid (*Gymnadenia odoratissima*) and the green-flowered helleborine (*Epipactis phyllanthes*). Other protected plants include the Gotland buttercup (*Ranunculus ophioglossifolius*), the Gotland cress (*Inula crassifolia*), the Karlsö

31

lettuce (*Lactuca quercina*), sea holly (*Eryngium maritimum*) and the Hartstongue fern (*Phyllitis scolopendrium*). The burnt tip, or dwarf, orchid (*Orchis ustulata*) is very common, and has no less than ten popular names. So is the early purple orchid (*Orchis mascula*), which is locally known, from the resemblance of its flowers to spiky primitive keys, as 'St Peter's Keys'. Most of the above, rare and common, flower in May and June, and are to be found in remote untouched habitats such as the heath near Hejnum, south-east of Tingstäde, or on Stora Karlsö.

Of the many other, more ordinary, flowers, among the most striking are the colourful tall ones—the clear blue chicory (*Chicorium intybus*), which is now so widespread, especially on the verges of roads, that has almost been adopted as the national flower of Gotland; viper's bugloss (*Echium vulgare*), very appropriately known in Swedish as 'blue fire'; and rose bay (*Epilobium angustifolium*), also appropriately known as 'fireweed'. The columbine (*Aquilegia vulgaris*), possibly a garden escape, has also in the last few decades established itself widely. Other flowers, individually smaller than the above but growing in tight drifts —the wood anemone (*Anemone nemorosa*) or the rarer pasque flower (*Pulsatilla vulgaris* var *Gotlandica*) and many others—add their contribution of brilliant and unforgettable colour.

Something over 1,000 different plants have been identified on Gotland. Compared with other regions of south Sweden, this is a low figure. In fact many plants common on the Swedish mainland opposite have not been found on Gotland at all. Interestingly enough, and as one would expect, the flora of the island of Öland is intermediate between that of the mainland and Gotland. The botanical importance of Gotland, however, is that, even if it has fewer species than neighbouring countries, it has a number unique in Northern Europe, and this includes various grasses and other plants of undistinguished aspect in addition to the flowers mentioned above.

Trees

The commonest tree on Gotland is the pine (*Pinus*). It is also the oldest. A piece of a pine tree preserved under sea-sand and pebbles has been established by radioactive methods of dating to be about 10,000 years old. Spruce (*Picea abies*) is the next commonest conifer and is abundant in the north of the island, where it grows unusually high. On some tracts of exposed and stony ground the small grey-green juniper (*Juniperus*) is found. On climatic grounds, as well as from the discovery of the piece of ancient pine mentioned above, these coniferous evergreens are considered to have taken root on the island considerably earlier than the various deciduous trees. The latter established themselves in the warm period of the Litorina Age and are a fairly standard mixture of species common in Northern Europe —birch, oak, ash (well enough known not to require botanical labels). The mountain ash, the rowan of Scotland (and *rönn* of Scandinavia) (*Sorbus aucuparia*), its cousin the wild service tree (*Sorbus terminalis*), comparatively rare in England, and the wych elm (*Ulmus glabra*) are quite often found, but alders (*Alnus*), limes or lindens (*Tilia*) and maples (*Acer*) less so. Most woods are of mixed species and pleasantly open, with a thick carpet of lush grass and flowers. There is often an undergrowth of hazel bushes (*Corylus*). A grassy glade, in either an evergreen or a deciduous wood, is a famous feature of Gotland where it is known as an *äng*. These clearings once covered much of the inhabited part of the island, giving it an idyllic park-like quality that captivated early visitors. *Ängar* played an important role in traditional husbandry as a rich source of hay, but have now been cleared in the interests of larger-scale methods of cultivation. Undisturbed through the centuries, they also did much to preserve the original flora. For this reason and also to retain a living piece of the past—not to mention their intrinsic beauty— some of them are now protected and maintained in their pristine state. There is one at Bunge Folk Museum.

In damp places in the more open country bog myrtle (*Myrica gale*) and various willows (*Salix* spp) are locally common. Visby's favourable site and the shelter afforded by high buildings and walled gardens allow trees and shrubs to flourish well north of their normal habitate, among them walnut, mulberry, peach and apricot. The Botanic Gardens (see p 120) exploit these advantages and contain several rare species.

FAUNA

Birds

For climatic and geological reasons Gotland has a rich bird life, both resident and migrant. There are razorbills (*Alca torda*) on Stora Karlsö and its large breeding colonies of guillemots (*Uria aalge*), including the black guillemot, have already been mentioned. There are other interesting seabirds, less noisy and less numerous, to be seen. To list them would be tedious, but a few do merit individual mention. The great black-backed gull (*Larus marinus*) and the little gull (*Larus minutus*), the largest and smallest of their species respectively, and several unusual terns—black tern (*Chlidonias niger*), Caspian tern (*Hydroprogne caspia*) and arctic tern (*Sterna macrura*)—flourish in Gotland with their more common brethren. Noteworthy among the ducks and larger aquatic birds are the scaup (*Aythya marila*), goldeneye (*Buchephala claugula*), smew (*Mergus albellus*), velvet scoter (*Melanitta fusca*) and ferruginous duck (*Aythya nyroca*); and there are red-breasted merganser (*Mergus serrator*), black-throated diver (*Colymbus arcticus*) and greylag goose (*Anser anser*).

Several very rare birds such as the black-tailed godwit (*Limosa limosa*) and the collared fly-catcher (*Muscicapa albicollis*) are protected. Other waders such as snipe and redshank are comparatively common, as are the more ordinary spotted and pied fly-catchers. Some birds not unusual in Scandinavia are of interest to visitors from other countries where they are seldom,

Page 35   Visby Cathedral, the biggest church on Gotland and the only one left of sixteen
in the city in the Middle Ages

Page 36 (*above*) A not untypical pastoral scene—Rute Church in its country setting; (*below*) one of the churches which were never finished. Vamlingbo with its stunted tower, a victim of the troubles of the late fourteenth century

if ever, seen. Among these may be cited that small brown crow, the nutcracker (*Nucifraga caryocatactes*), the big black woodpecker (*Dryocopus martius*) with its red crest, the waxwing (*Bombicilla garrulus*) and wryneck (*Jynx torquilla*). Birds of prey are quite numerous and varied. They include the goshawk (*Accipiter gentilis*) buzzard (*Buteo buteo*), lesser spotted eagle (*Aquila pomarina*) and golden eagle (*Aquila chrysäetos*). From the various tits, warblers, finches and assorted other birds the following are worth watching for, as all may from time to time be seen on Gotland: barred warbler (*Sylvia nisoria*), icterine warbler (*Hippolais icterina*), roller (*Coracia garrulus*) and purple sandpiper (*Calidris maritima*). The thrush nightingale (*Luscinia luscinia*), East European cousin of Keats' 'immortal bird', may be heard in the appropriate season; and various game birds may be shot, mainly black grouse (*Lyurus tetrix*), introduced a couple of hundred years ago, willow grouse and pheasants, also introduced for sport, at the end of the nineteenth century.

Animals and Fishes

The small sturdy Gotland pony, very like the widely known Shetland pony, is the most interesting animal among the comparatively few found on the island. It is known as *russ*—a word which, through the Old Norse *hross*, is closely connected to the English 'horse', and is quite different from the Swedish word for the animal (*häst*). There is also a local breed of small cow. Rabbits were introduced early this century (being known in the local language as *rabbis*) and have become a pest, although temporarily checked by myxomatosis a couple of decades or so ago. Hares are fairly common. Roe deer may be encountered in open woodlands. There are also foxes, squirrels, several sorts of snakes and the usual small animals.

Seals, descendants of the once numerous packs that played so important a role in the Gotlandic economy for thousands of years, can still be seen on remote parts of the coast. These are mainly the grey seal (*Halichoerus grypus*), with some bearded seals (*Erignathus barbatus*). The commonest fishes are the Baltic herring, the delicious small *strömming* which tastes like flying-fish; cod; flounder (dab), which when smoked becomes a local speciality; and, in season, salmon. There is good fishing in some of the 'meres' for the usual freshwater fish of the region —pike, roach, dace and so forth.

3   THE FIRST INHABITANTS

T HE oldest remains of human habitation on Gotland are in the north-east. Flint chippings and fragments of bone have been found in fire-charred deposits in the district around Gothem (in itself an appropriate name for the site of the first settlement, since it means 'Home of the Goths'). These, like the discoveries on Stora Karlsö already mentioned, belong to the Late Stone Age and are about 7,000 years old. Tradition states that the first man to land on Gotland was called Tjelvar. The island at the time was in the power of evil spirits who caused it to sink by day and rise by night. When Tjelvar lit a fire, the spell was broken and the island remained above the waves. The story of a 'sinking island' is geologically correct. It is also correct that the earliest remains of man's presence so far discovered on Gotland in which evidence of fire is important are in just that part of it where Tjelvar is said to have landed. Tradition appears to be recounting actual events. It may even be that the leader of the first important group of settlers really was called Tjelvar. He may even have looked like the shaggy dolls the tourist shops sell. But he certainly had no connection with the important ship-grave in this district known as 'Tjelvar's Grave', because this is a Bronze Age monument of several thousand years later.

These Stone Age men, however, did leave enough evidence of their activities to place them in history. They were great seal hunters, and used the teeth of the animals they had eaten for dress—if a 'Bikini' skirt of seal teeth can properly be so called—and adornment, the teeth being pierced and strung on a thong to make a necklace. They maintained links across the Baltic both with southern Scandinavia from near Visby and to the south and east from near Gothem, where the excavation of an important side at Västerbjärs in the 1930s provided much information on their habits. They traded in the beautiful stone axeheads characteristic of the Later Stone Age in Northern Europe. At Hall, right in the north of the island, they also made their own; and a veritable axehead factory has been unearthed there. Unlike the people they were in touch with in South Sweden and Denmark, they did not build the cromlechs (chamber tombs) characteristic of this era, though there are numerous small burial cairns from this time. The evidence of regular intercourse provides fascinating proof that even in those far distant days the Gotlanders had realised, and were exploiting, the commercial advantages of their central position in the Baltic.

THE BRONZE AGE

In the Bronze Age (from about 1500 to 500 BC) Gotland became a flourishing and prosperous community with its face to the sea. To the west was the dominant local culture of Denmark and South Sweden, avid for amber from the Baltic middlemen on Gotland. To the south and east were other peoples with whom good business could be done. Behind them in Central Europe lay the restless Indo-Germanic tribes, with links to Asia and the Mediterranean and new ideas, and, above all, knowledge of the gleaming new metal that gives its name to this age.

The improvement in the climate at this period must have helped Gotland's development. The land was more bountiful and living easier in softer weather. Indeed the puzzling absence of any remains of strong houses has led many experts to conclude that the weather was so clement that there was no need for them. The superiority of tools made of bronze instead of flints or antlers could have reinforced this trend. Like many primitive tribes today in suitable climates the ancient Gotlanders might have cleared the ground for a season or two only and then, since implements of the new metal made the work so much easier, moved on to start again when the land was exhausted. Such speculation, at any rate, goes far to explain why men who could erect the monuments these ancient Gotlanders have left behind, thus demonstrating their ability to build permanent stone dwellings had they thought fit, have left no traces of habitation.

What they have left are their remarkable tombs. The effort and organisation required to produce them manifestly reflects a prosperous community, well organised and with ample resources. It is not too fanciful—particularly in view of the Mediterranean affinities mentioned below—to consider the Bronze Age men of Gotland similar in organisation and habits to the Heroes described in Homer's great poems—the 'fair-haired Achaeans' did after all come down to Greece from the north. They also cremated their dead and buried the ashes in urns, as the Gotlanders began to do soon after the Bronze Age began.

Their whole attitude to death implies a remarkable growth of religious consciousness at this time. The ship-graves, which are no puny patterns of assorted stones but graceful constructions up to 140ft long, with high prows, raking lines and solid sterns, may, as some have suggested, reflect the influence of the Sun Ships of the ancient Egyptians. The great cairns may have been northern counterparts of the Pyramids or, more plausibly, the beehive tomb of Agamemnon at Mycenae. The very few cairns examined so far do in fact shown evidence of a columnar, or a domed, central chamber. Also a bronze sword of a type familiar at Troy has come to light on Gotland. Obviously no connection with Greece can be firmly postulated, but what is certain is that there are today on Gotland more significantly older and usually bigger Bronze Age ship-graves and cairns than anywhere else.

GOTLAND

Cairns

On the island there are about 400 'Big Cairns' (called in the Gotlandic tongue *Rojr*, or in Swedish *Rös*; both may be seen on maps). Some are quite low and those that have been investigated have had low, well built, drystone retaining walls inside—like the later and smaller Iron Age graves discussed below. Others now appear as enormous mounds of stones, the biggest (*Uggarde Rojr*) on the south-east coast near Rone being 140ft in diameter and 25ft high. Few of these big cairns have been examined, and none completely. The first recorded investigation was of *Angantyrs Rojr* a few miles south of Uggarde by the local parson in the early nineteenth century. He found evidence of a circular chamber which had collapsed (some of these big cairns have a depression in the centre and are known locally as 'crater-cairns': the collapse of the actual burial chamber would produce just this effect); and right in the middle of the great pile of stones he found a small stone coffin containing a cremation and a fine dagger of the Early Bronze Age. In the few sites of this nature which they have examined to date better qualified investigators have confirmed these early findings. For example, at Grauns, near Lärbro in the north, the remains of a similar central wall of dressed stone were found.

Stone Ships

The other memorable Bronze Age monuments on Gotland are the tombs in the shape of stone ships—properly built by men who knew and loved ships. In fact, though it would be unwise to press the point, a case could be made out for distinguishing the graves of warriors, with long narrow warships, from those of merchants, with proportionately beamier craft. The largest of 350 or so memorials of this type is a lovely long ship-grave at Gnisvärd, just off the main coast road about 12 miles south of Visby, which is 140ft long and 23ft wide. Another big tomb at Gannarve, a few miles farther south, is approxi-

42

mately 96ft long and 15ft wide. Their proportions, with a length
to breadth ratio of about six or seven to one, are surprisingly
similar to those of later Viking warships. Elsewhere, as at
Rannarve east of Klintehamn and between the two sites mentioned above, smaller, broader ships are delineated by the
memorial stones. Here in fact there are four in line ahead,
each one 30ft by 13ft and considerably deeper, as befits a
merchantman which must earn its keep.

In other places ship-graves and cairns are found together,
notably at Galrum near the east coast just inland from Ljugarn.
Sometimes monuments of much later times, such as 'picture-
stones' (p 46), are also found on what through the ages had
remained holy ground.

A few ship-graves of considerably later date are to be seen in
districts on the south Baltic coast which are known to have had
close connexions with Gotland—in Bornholm or South Sweden,
or in Estonia and Latvia. It is generally accepted that they are
derived from those on Gotland. The amazing thing is that, on
an island in the middle of the Baltic, so many highly developed
monuments of a very special type appeared so early. The con-
cept of the soul journeying to its last resting place beyond the
western sea in a great ship is widespread. It survived in Scandinavia until the Vikings were converted to Christianity and, as
every schoolboy knows, their chiefs used to set off on their last
voyage in a blazing longship. Rock drawings probably depicting
the same rite in the days before the Vikings are found in
southern Norway. There is at least one also in Gotland, at
Hägvide, near Lärbro; but the typically Gotlandic memorial
is a big ship constructed of carefully aligned stones.

For the rest nothing of outstanding merit from the Bronze
Age has been found on the island. There are many good examples of what might be called the standard artefacts—swords,
daggers, jewellery and articles of dress such as brooches and
shoulder-pins for cloaks. There is the intriguing sword of a
Trojan type. But the most impressive piece of bronze is a

magnificent Roman cauldron, probably of the first century of our era, which, with so many other treasures, may be seen in the Museum at Visby.

THE IRON AGE

There is to date insufficient evidence to permit a coherent account to be given of the transition, about 500 BC, from the Bronze Age to the Iron Age on Gotland. A site near Visby airport, at Annelund, is being excavated at the time of writing for the fourth successive year in the hope of shedding light on this dark and rather confused period. It is already known that there was, about 500 BC, a sudden, indeed a catastrophic, deterioration in the climate in Northern Europe. Iron-hard weather ushered in the Iron Age. The glittering sun-loving culture of the Bronze Age, so to speak, froze in its grip and quite rapidly withered away. Yet, paradoxically, it seems that the new people, or at any rate the new culture, also came to Gotland from farther south, probably from the Celts in Central Europe. The Gotlanders, who by 200 BC were smelting their own iron, were ahead of mainland Scandinavia in this—which implies that they were nearer the source of the new ideas and thus received them earlier.

The people who brought iron also brought new burial customs. In place of the long stone ships and the high cairns we find from this pre-Roman Iron Age small low mounds with neat retaining walls. Beneath the covering of earth and stones, graves from this period occasionally have doubtless mystical patterns of small stones in concentric circles or radiating from a central point like the spokes of a wheel. (Both these patterns are found on older stone monuments in Western Europe and the Mediterranean.) The dead are now buried, not burnt, and their potent iron weapons go with them to the after life. Just who these newcomers were and how they were able to overthrow the long-established culture of the Bronze Age is a mystery. We

44

know from elsewhere—from Egypt, for example—how swiftly invaders with iron weapons vanquished troops armed with the softer bronze; but we do not know whether the new metal and new customs were brought to Gotland by invaders, or accepted by the existing inhabitants as the products of a superior civilisation.

The Roman Iron Age

From about the beginning of the Christian era until well into the fifth century Gotland flourished mightily. The island's position enabled it to profit from a lively entrepôt trade with the wealthy Roman Empire. Links to the western provinces ran through Gothic kinsmen in Germany. To the east also there were well trodden paths to the Black Sea and Byzantium, with settlements of kith and kin en route. As a result about two-thirds of all the Roman coins of this period, mainly silver *denarii*, found in the whole of Scandinavia have been found on Gotland. So many other Roman products dug up from graves or found by chance—the magnificent bronze cauldron mentioned earlier, drinking bowls, wine ladles, typical Roman glass and beads and a host of other articles—tell the same story of thriving trade and close connexions that this period is known to archaeologists in Northern Europe as the Roman Iron Age.

Much of the above material has come from graves, where it represents the dead owner's most prized possessions, left to serve him in eternity. Often there are weapons, but these are locally made. Local, too, are the carefully shaped throwing stones for the ancient game of *varpa*, which several graves—doubtless of some champions in the sport, or at any rate enthusiasts—have yielded up. There are very many graves from this time: indeed it is this period which is largely responsible for the fact that out of about 31,000 known sites of historical interest on Gotland about 25,000 are graves at no less than 880 cemeteries. Some of the later cemeteries, ie some of those which continued in use up to the end of the period, are very large indeed, with thousands of individual graves. Among the most noteworthy are those at Lilla Bjärs east of Stenkyrka about 15 miles north of Visby; Trullhalsar in the centre of the east coast; and Barshaldars south-east of Grötlingbo, in the south.

Early Picture-stones

Towards the end of the Roman Iron Age, about AD 400, a new, and another distinctively Gotlandic, form of monument appeared. This was the 'picture-stone' (*bildsten*), of which about 300 have been found on the island. They are of two main types—an earlier simpler monument in the shape of an axehead with curved blade uppermost; and a later type (discussed in Chapter 4), much larger, taller and proportionately narrower, with a semicircular 'mushroom' head not unlike the shape of the headstone of many Christian graves in subsequent ages. The axe was—and in some primitive cultures still is—a mystic symbol of great power. It appears in the Minoan civilisation of Crete, and it was certainly symbolic of authority to the Romans. More practically the battleaxe was the select weapon of the Norsemen several hundred years later, and it armed the picked band of Harold's bodyguard at the Battle of Hastings. So, in the light of the known cult of the axe in many different places at many different times, it is not surprising to find evidence of it on an island with such widespread and distant connexions with other cultures as Gotland. What is surprising is that, like the ship-graves, it should spring up in the form of these picture-stones quite suddenly and without any obvious antecedents.

The early picture-stones have simple but elegant geometrical patterns, and mystic symbols such as the 'Sun-Wheel' or 'Wheel of Life'. Horses with elongated bodies, reminiscent of the 'White Horses' cut in the chalk at various places in England and known to have had a religious significance for the old Germanic peoples, are also common, usually in pairs apparently fighting.

The designs also include worm-like dragons, or serpents—
another common symbol of these early Northern tribes. Among
others the Visby Museum has a very good example of an early
stone from Havor, near Hablingbo in the south; and this also
shows traces of having been painted in strong primary colours.
Another good picture-stone, and one of the oldest, is built into
the tower of Bro Church. Additional motifs on these fascinating
memorials are various animals, men and boats, including big
rowing boats without a sail. In this latter respect both the early
and the late stones provide valuable evidence for the study of
early ships.

'Giants' Graves'

This same period has also left the evidence of the first permanent buildings on Gotland. The remains of nearly 1,500 houses
and huts have been mapped, usually near the sites of *ängar* (see
p 33), now destroyed, and along the shores of ancient meres,
now drained. They consist of low walls of stone in a rectangular
shape, with rounded corners, and are usually in small groups.
At Vallhagar, however, near Fröjel, in the south, there is a
large settlement of twenty-four houses, and it is from the
thorough excavation of this site that much of our detailed
knowledge of these buildings, and the life of their inhabitants,
has come. Of the hundreds of other sites of this kind only a few
dozen have been examined, but the story they tell confirms the
conclusions based on the painstaking work over several seasons
at Vallhagar. Very few artefacts of great intrinsic value have so
far been found among the ruins of the Roman Iron Age houses.
Archaeologically speaking, however, the bits of pottery, the
fragments of cloth, the whetstones, the spindle-whorls and
other mundane objects form a useful complement to the
weapons and other more highly valued relics the graves of this
period have provided.

It is assumed that these low walls supported the sloping
beams that formed the roof of these houses—a type of building

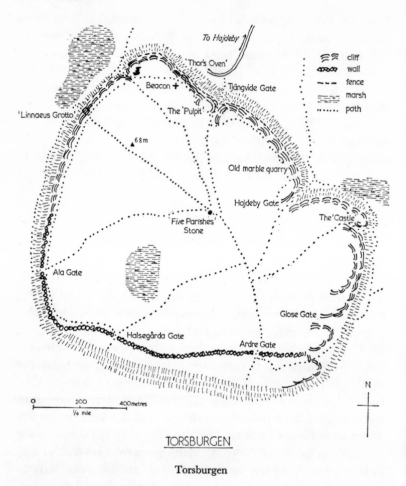

cliff
wall
fence
marsh
path

To Hajdeby

'Thor's Oven'

Tjängvide Gate

Beacon

The 'Pulpit'

'Linnaeus Grotto'

68 m

Old marble quarry

Hajdeby Gate

The 'Castle'

Five Parishes Stone

Ala Gate

Glose Gate

Halsegårda Gate

Ardre Gate

0   200   400 metres

¼ mile

N

TORSBURGEN

Torsburgen

depicted on the later picture-stones and otherwise well known.
(A reconstruction of one of these houses may be seen at Lojstahallen a few miles east of Lojsta, about 25 miles from Visby on
the main road to the south.) The shape and size of these remains
have earned for them the name of 'Giants' Graves' among the
Gotlanders. The settlements so far examined nearly all show
signs of fire and violent destruction at a date put by the experts

48

at the second half of the fifth century. This was a time of great unrest, when the Roman Empire in the west was collapsing. So it is not surprising that Gotland bears the marks of homes destroyed. The number of graves dating from this unsettled era is also much smaller than for the immediately preceding centuries.

There is also in the *Gutasaga* a much discussed passage which, whatever the exact significance or origin of particular phrases, is now generally accepted to refer to the depopulation of Gotland at this time, and the flight of its inhabitants to strong points or to possibly safer lands across the sea. It specifically mentions that a group that did not want to leave the island 'went up to Torsburgen'. Here still stand the remains of the biggest fort in Scandinavia, a mixture of natural protection afforded by rock cliffs and man-made walls enclosing an area over a mile across. There are in fact about seventy forts on Gotland from these restless times. Some are on the tops of hills such as Torsburgen or Styrmansberget (near Fröjel). Others, like Binge Slott ('Binge Castle'), near Väte in the middle of the island, are raised earthworks with defensive ditches. But all bear witness to the end of an age.

4   *THE VIKINGS*

THE Viking Age is generally reckoned to have lasted for some 250 years, from about AD 800. The first recorded raid on England was in 787. In the summer of 793 the rich and defenceless monastery of Lindisfarne off the Northumbrian coast was plundered and the monks slaughtered by a war-band from across the sea. Thereafter the raiders returned year after year, ranging ever more widely along the coast of Western Europe and thrusting ever more deeply inland. From about 850 they began to over-winter in the lands they attacked and finally established kingdoms there. On a smaller scale in Scandinavia itself this movement, due to the pressure of over-population on limited local resources, started somewhat earlier than the violent overseas expansion to distant lands that the very word Viking connotes. For Gotland it meant the acceptance of the sovereignty of the King of the Svea across the sea in Central Sweden, and a great upsurge of trade as old routes were expanded and new ones opened up by the adventurous Norsemen.

What happened is again recorded in the *Gutasaga* in what again is accepted by modern historians as a basically accurate account. It states that, after 'many kings' had attacked Gotland unsuccessfully, the Gotlanders of their own accord sent an envoy to the Swedish king and put themselves under his protection, agreeing to make an annual payment of 60 silver marks in return for what would now be called reciprocal free trade facilities. The Saga, accurate on events and people, is vague on dates, but the consensus of expert opinion holds that this momentous development occurred about the middle of the sixth century.

THE ENTREPÔT OF EASTERN TRADE

With their safety and commercial rights thus guaranteed, the Gotlanders concentrated on building up the lucrative trade assured to them by their favourable position in the Baltic, remaining rather apart from the main political developments in North-Western Europe in the next few centuries. Their main trade was with Byzantium and the prosperous Arab realms of Western Asia, whose silver mines financed the trade of the known world. The runic inscription on an eleventh-century whetstone succinctly records the situation. 'Ulvar Ormika [the names of two Vikings] Greece [the Byzantine Empire] Jerusalem Iceland Arabia' it says, commemorating the travels of its owners and dramatically symbolising the range of Gotland's interests at the time.

The Vikings developed their northern routes to replace the Mediterranean ones blocked by the mutual hostility of Christian West and Muslim East. Religious differences ironically gave them another advantage. As Foote and Wilson put it: 'Human beings were probably the commonest commodity the Vikings dealt in, both as traders and raiders.' The Arabs had an insatiable demand for slaves but Christians were prohibited from selling them (at least to heathen customers). No such scruples hampered the Norsemen, who dragged off impartially both distant Christians and Scandinavian neighbours to sell for profit. They also sold furs and weapons to the Eastern lands, receiving in payment silver coins (*dirhams*), of which over 60,000 (about a quarter of the total found in northern Europe) have come to light on Gotland, the centre of this trade. Thus, in a less monopolistic form Gotland in the ninth and tenth centuries achieved a pre-eminence in East-West trade comparable to that of Venice a couple of hundred years later. The Got-

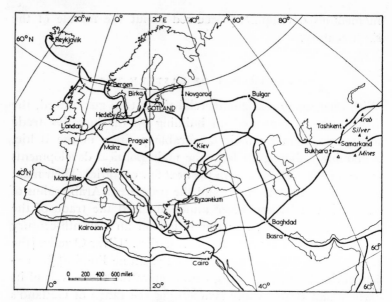

Viking trade routes

landers' familiarity with Christianity before their conversion was attributed as a matter of course in the Saga to their contact with the many pilgrims visiting the island—'For at that time the way to Jerusalem and Greece was through Gotland.'

Very little is known of Gotland's trade with the West in the Viking Age. The inscription quoted above indicates contacts with Iceland, which is not at all surprising. Towards the end of the period coins from Western Europe in general, and from the tenth-century England of Ethelred the Unready in particular, predominate. But this was as much because the Arabian mines had by then been worked out and various western silver coinages (of metal from new mines in Saxony) had replaced the *dirhams* in international trade as because the Gotlanders at this time had increased their trade with the West.

Page 53 (*right*) A good example of the Gotlandic Gothic style, Gothem Church, built by 'Egypticus' in the thirteenth century, seen through an elegant gate in the fortified wall to the churchyard; (*below*) the mighty sculptures of the porch of Stånga Church, the magnificent but here ill-balanced work of Gotland's master-builder 'Egypticus'

Page 54 Interiors: (above) The magnificent thirteenth-century rood in Öja Church, a masterpiece of Gothic wood-carving; (below) mixed styles in Hejdeby Church. Most of the frescoes seen are from the thirteenth century, but the two lower ones on the right (St George and St Martin) are by the fifteenth-century 'Master of the Passion'. The small rood is early thirteenth century

ART, ORNAMENT AND CRAFTS

The culture of Gotland was Viking with important local variations. As with the ship-graves of the Bronze Age or the earliest picture-stones, so now in certain fields of applied art the Gotlanders, on present evidence, were again innovators. In particular the series of beautifully designed and brilliantly executed gilt-bronze bridle-mounts from Broa, in Halla parish in the middle of the island, is reckoned by experts to be the finest known example of the earliest Viking decorative style as well as one of the most splendid finds from the whole Viking Age. There are three main motifs on these objects, all composed of twisted animals with small heads and frond-like limbs, the body being impossibly elongated or foreshortened to fit the space to be decorated. The homogeneity of style and execution has led to the conclusion that these pieces were the work of one man— 'The Master Jeweller of Broa'—in the first half of the ninth century. It is interesting to see how early the involved abstract animal patterns, so typical of later Viking and Celtic art, were developed on Gotland—and with what consummate skill.

Of the many other examples of Viking metal craft, in gold for adornment or in base metals for use, the most interesting is the bronze vane (burgee) from a ship of about AD 1000, a copy of which may now be seen in Källunge Church, where until quite recently the original had served for centuries as a weathercock. The style of its decoration is derived from that developed in the Ringerike district in Norway, north of Oslo, which is both a graceful culmination of earlier turgid styles and, particularly in Southern England and Ireland, the precursor of a widespread native idiom. Gold jewellery of great beauty has also been found on Gotland—bracelets, torques, bracteates, beads and so forth—as well as such things as ornamented scabbard-mounts and sword-grips.

With the exception of the wooden 'stave-church' from

Hemse, which is now in the Historical Museum in Stockholm, all the significant artistic finds of this period have been in metal or stone. The Gotlanders obviously used ships, but there are no spectacular remains like those from Gokstad or Oseberg in Norway, with their magnificent intricate decoration and skilful construction. An interesting and homely minor find of considerable technological importance was that of a Viking carpenter's tool chest in the swampy ground of Mästermyr, with a very full array of tools—axe, adze, saws, spoon-bit, assorted auger bits and other recognisable implements. Much light is also shed on articles of everyday use from carts to ships and weapons by their portrayal on contemporary picture-stones.

Late Picture-stones

The picture-stones that reached the peak of their development in the eighth century are quite different from the earlier type. They are generally much larger—up to 10ft in height—and shaped like narrow 'button mushrooms'. More important is the fact that they narrate in pictures a complex story rather than display largely abstract mystical symbols. To the men of the age the pictures almost certainly had some symbolic significance which is lost to us, but this is contained in scenes of readily identifiable everyday activities. Not surprisingly in view of the turbulent times ships and fighting are their commonest motifs. The whole subject of these stones, both late and early, has been exhaustively treated in Prof Sune Lindquist's monumental work *Gotlands Bildsteine*, but it is worth stressing here their importance as a mine of information on the history of ship development at the critically important period of transition from rowing to sailing in the northern seas. There is parallel evidence from the numerous buried ships found mainly in Norway, and from rock drawings outside Gotland; but, again, the material from Gotland tends to be earlier and, therefore, of special significance.

A quite superficial examination of the convenient selection of picture-stones in Gotlands Fornsal or the open-air museum at Bunge shows many thought-provoking features. The sailing boats have the typical square Viking sail (still seen in Western Norway and, until recent years, on the Yorkshire coast). Either the decoration or the fabrication of the sail (or both) is clearly shown with contrasting squares of dark and light material. From the bottom of some sails descends a tangle of ropes, which are thought to show that the sail could be reefed. Similarly the sheets fastened to the ends of the boom on several drawings could mean that the sail could be swung out of its standard position, thus enabling the ship to sail closer to the wind than is often assumed. The great steering-oar (the 'steer-board', or 'starboard') is clearly shown at the stern. There are little ships with only two or three crew, and there are grim warships with lines of shields on their gunwales, piles of spears at the prow, bearded warriors with helmets and the dreaded dragon figure-head.

On land—or is it in Valhalla?—there is much fighting on foot and on horseback, with broadswords, spears and occasionally battleaxes. Too true a picture of the times is given by the vignettes on several stones of stockaded farmhouses under attack. Among the more peaceful pursuits shown are fish-spearing; driving along in a cart with four solid wheels, a dog yapping and wagging his tail in front; or two elks rubbing noses.

Other scenes, whatever their exact interpretation, are far more sinister. On a big stone from Lärbro a man is clearly shown hanging from a tree while nearby a trussed bird (probably a swan) is being laid on an altar. There are other men and objects in the scene, which seems to depict the sort of regular sacrificial ritual recorded from other Viking lands. In particular, Master Adam of Bremen, the eleventh-century monk and chronicler, describes in gruesome detail the sacrifice of male animals (including men by hanging) in the sacred grove at

Uppsala, the capital of the Svea kingdom. Other scenes, showing hovering birds and women carrying wreaths, usually near a prone body, are reasonably assumed to depict Valkyries taking to Valhalla the soul of the fallen warrior, whose memorial the stone presumably is, just as the carvings on late Roman tombstones or the pictures in an Egyptian tomb show the progress, and the prowess, of the dead men they commemorate.

Towards the end of this later period the decorations on the 'picture-stones' change completely. Crosses appear in the rounded head, the contorted elongated animal motifs typical of later Viking art replace the crowded narrative scenes, and runic inscriptions twist round the borders in place of the former intertwined 'rope-work'. The whole effect is much more modern and more familiar, because the later stones resemble the medieval Christian gravestones widely seen in North-Western Europe.

The conversion of Gotland to Christianity was effected by the Norwegian King Olaf Haraldsson in 1029. The arrival at Akergarn on the north-east coast of St Olaf on a crusade to Russia is traditionally associated with the sudden and forceful conversion of the Gotlanders to Christianity. The Norwegians' arrival must have marked the culmination of earlier developments, when Botair built the first churches at Vi (almost certainly Visby), Stenkyrka and Kulstäde. The presence of a well armed expeditionary force of the same faith, however, no doubt tipped the balance in favour of the Christian faction.

In the event Olaf became the patron saint of Gotland, Akergarn was renamed St Olofshamn, and Christianity made rapid progress. For some time paganism and Christianity existed side by side, as earlier, but now Christianity was dominant. Whatever traces of heathen beliefs and practices remained (and, as usual in country districts, probably still do) as unwitting superstitions, dismissed with a laugh, or disguised in a Christian wrapping, the frequent bloody sacrifices at least were ended. 'They offered in sacrifice their sons and daughters and beasts, also food and drink', records the *Gutasaga*. But now the similarly ancient and authoritative code of Gotlandic law, the *Gutalagen*, uncompromisingly states: 'This is the first article of our law, that we shall say No to heathendom and Yes to Christianity and all believe in Almighty God and pray to Him for help.'

A THOUSAND YEAR SOCIETY

Far-reaching political changes were also wrought by the Vikings on Gotland. They laid the foundations of a self-governing oligarchy of farmer-traders which lasted nearly 1,000 years and has left indelible marks on the life of the island and the character of the islanders. The basis of the system was the *ding* (now known as *ting*), the assembly of free men. The national assembly, the *Gutnalding* (the 'Council of all the Goths'), was held at Roma, well placed in the centre of the island. Below this body the island was divided into three parts, each with a *treding* (a name perpetuated in England in the three 'Ridings' of Yorkshire), and below these again were smaller district councils. This basic system, common to other Viking lands, has made a vital contribution to parliamentary democracy in Europe and North America. Its social basis was a system of large estates centred on a big farm where 100 or more people commonly lived—the sort of 'long-house' organisation found in societies where the men are often away. These estates continued almost in their original form until the late seventeenth century, when they were broken up by the introduction of new systems of taxation and land tenure from Sweden proper after Gotland was incorporated in Sweden by the Peace of Bromsebro in 1645. Nevertheless, as may be seen from a modern map, the names of many of them are still retained by the smaller modern holdings.

So, as the modern world evolved in the early Middle Ages after the upsurge of expansion, raids and the founding of kingdoms, Gotland found itself in a particularly favourable position to benefit from the unprecedented prosperity of Western Europe in the years between the end of the Viking Age and the disastrous onslaught, in the mid-fourteenth century, of the Black Death. Its key position in the lucrative trade between West and East was well established. At home there was a stable community with close ties of kinship and faith with major customers abroad. Even the climate had improved; and in both senses the sun began to shine on Gotland's Golden Age.

5   THE GOLDEN AGE

FOR 300 years from the middle of the eleventh century Gotland flourished as never before or since. Visby was one of the great cities of Europe, comparable in importance and riches to London or Paris, and marked in purple and gold on the maps of Florence. Its population of about 40,000 was almost twice that of the present city, and that of the countryside must have been at least as large as today's. The Sea Laws of Visby were the foundation of modern maritime law. Official purveyors of 'minever and wax' to the kings of England, the Gotlanders signed treaties with the dukes of Novgorod, Henry the Lion, Duke of Saxony, and other rulers as equals. They sent embassies to Bruges and to Byzantium and maintained trading-posts in thirty or so other commercial centres like Riga, Lübeck or London—where the financial probity of the 'men from the East' (Easterlings) was perpetuated in the British 'sterling' currency. Small wonder then that Chaucer, who was Comptroller of Customs in London before he fell into royal disfavour and took to writing poetry, in the Prologue to the *Canterbury Tales* illustrated the experience of his Skipper by reference to his familiarity with

> . . . all the havens as they were
> From Gotland to the Cape of Finisterre.

How prosperous Gotland then was is very evident today. The first glimpse of the spectacular walls of Visby, crowned by the cathedral's towers, the pointed ruins of other great churches and the red-roofed step-gabled houses of wealthy medieval merchants, gives an impression of former riches and vanished glory that haunts one throughout the island. The villages were then so rich that they could build parish churches which are among the treasures of ecclesiastical architecture. The farmhouses, too, the heart of the society described in Chapter 4, reflected a thriving community. Several have survived in good repair—Kattlunds, an early example in the south; and the later Stora Hästnäs, a few miles north-east of Visby. There is nothing like them anywhere else in Scandinavia (except for a few buildings copied from them). Kattlunds in particular is like the old farms in Corsica or Sicily or the Pennine district in the north of England. Stora Hästnäs, smaller and higher, and having marked defensive features, reminds one of a 'keep' in the once restless Border country between England and Scotland. Many of these buildings survived until the introduction of new methods of farming 100 odd years ago led to their destruction. Early travellers who visited them spoke of them in awe as a combination of palace and fort. Indeed they had to be when the riches of Gotland were a permanent lure to Baltic marauders. Hence we also find from this period, mainly in the south, a number of solidly built towers (known as *kastaler*, castles), usually serving no doubt as watch towers, but strong enough, and designed for, refuge and defence. Some churches also have defensive features.

The remains of the remarkable lake fort in Tingstäde Lake, so far as can be ascertained, date to the early part of this period. Known as 'The Bulwark' (*Bulverket*), it consists of a palissade some 200yd square with open water in the centre. It is constructed of thousands of stout posts and has been estimated to have taken at least 100,000 man-days to build. It was thoroughly investigated between the wars and there is a model of it in Burmeister House. Its general outline can be seen from the shore of the lake and, of course, much more from a boat above it.

The evidence of literature and legend, though fragmentary,

confirms the story of the stones. Chaucer's comments from England have been given above. An Italian, Tomasso Porcacci, in a study of the islands of the world published in 1577 speaks thus of Gotland:

> Gotlandia, an island in the Gothic Sea. . . . In the north is a city called Visby. . . . . Here come so many merchants that a similar entrepôt could scarcely be found in the whole of Europe.

Even allowing for the author's predilection for islands, this statement is inaccurate at the time he was writing, and must have been based on information relating to the period now under discussion.

The best known description of Gotland's affluence in this Golden Age is in the popular saw (which rhymes in the original) quoted by Hans Strelow, a Danish priest on Gotland, in his rather fanciful *Chronicle of the Gotlanders* (*Chronica Guthilandorum*), published in 1633. His version runs: 'The Gotlanders have so much gold they cannot weigh it. Their pigs eat from silver troughs. Their women spin with golden distaffs.' The nineteenth-century romantic school of medieval historians made great play with this description and (quite erroneously) considered that it was an important factor in the decision of the Danish King Valdemar Atterdag, to attack Gotland in 1361 with the aim of getting his hands on the treasures of the island.

The Gotlanders' own account in the *Gutasaga* is more concerned with the history of the island than its contemporary wealth. In old documents—treaties, trading charters, and so forth—there is more, scattered evidence of the importance of Gotland and the extent of her commercial interests. It is known, for example, that in London the Visby merchants had their own depot near the present Blackfriars Bridge. But there is no evidence at all for the remarkable view put forward by a seventeenth-century Bishop of Visby that Gotland was Atlantis.

GOTLAND

A DIVIDED COMMUNITY

For the first part of Gotland's Golden Age the old patterns of trade and politics persisted. Ports like Västergarn or Burgsvik, conveniently near the estates of the dominant merchant-farmers at a time when land transport was a difficult and time-consuming business, handled most of the island's trade. Though owing nominal allegiance to the Swedish king, the Gotlanders retained their ancient form of government and effective independence. The three established classes of society, reminiscent of later feudalism—the big landowners, the landless but free villeins, and the thralls, who were virtual slaves—maintained a system of self-government which avoided the permanent concentration of power in any one man's hands. The local councils functioned under the National Assembly, the elected chairman of which was for his turn of office the leader of this peasant republic. There was never a ruling aristocratic class on Gotland; nor did the dignitaries of the church wield political power. Gotland in fact was in the See of Linköping, across the water on the Swedish mainland, but its bishop set foot on the island only about once every 3 years.

So the Gotlanders prospered, the leading traders in Northern Europe. For a while they had the field to themselves but, in 1143, the city of Lübeck was founded on the North German coast, and behind it was the growing might of the Duchy of Saxony under its energetic ruler, Henry the Lion. The German merchants began to compete in the Gotlanders' territory and there was trouble. In 1161 the Germans took a significant step forward when the 'merchants of the Gotlandic coast' had to conclude with Duke Henry an agreement which, in return for the continuance of their trading rights in North Germany, granted the men of Lübeck reciprocal facilities on Gotland; and this move led to Lübeck's eventual supremacy. Visby now had the advantage of being a free port; but it also attracted foreign merchants with a tighter organisation and more modern methods than those traditionally employed by the individualistic farmer-traders of Gotland.

In the long run conflict between the thrusting efficient Germans and the Gotlanders was inevitable. Meanwhile 'the Society of Germans travelling to Gotland', with Visby as its headquarters and many Gotlanders in its ranks, became in the thirteenth century the most important trading group in Northern Europe, perpetuating for a few decades the island's ancient commercial supremacy. By 1229 eight towns belonged to this Society, and by the end of the century over thirty, Visby being the most important. The two component parts were always distinct. There was a Gotlandic, and a German, mayor of Visby, both countries were equally represented on the City Council, and the official description of the city in legal documents was 'the Gotlanders and Germans in Visby'. At the same time, in addition to internal rivalries in the city itself, Visby was increasingly at loggerheads with the rest of the island, whose trade it began to monopolise. Foreseeing trouble, the burghers of Visby, about the middle of the thirteenth century, built the city wall which still encompasses it.

In 1288 the expected civil war broke out, and the countrymen were defeated. The tomb of one of their leaders, Peter Harding, may still be seen with its appropriate inscription in Vall Church. But the fighting brought in the Swedish King Magnus Ladulås, to lay down the terms of peace. Thus reminded of his ancient rights in Gotland, he began increasingly to assert them: he made the burghers of Visby beg his pardon for having fortified their town without his permission, then fined them 2,000 silver marks, and raised the countrymen's taxes.

In historical perspective this fateful year marks the beginning of Gotland's decline. It was still very prosperous but was now on the periphery rather than at the centre of North European trade. It still had a great local importance, not least for its links with Russia, whence came raw materials much in demand. Good profits were made from Russian goods and from broadcloth, salt, ale and salt fish from farther west, not to mention the trade in small but valuable amounts of exotic wares—spices from Africa and the East Indies; rice, almonds and sugar from Spain; or wines from Bordeaux and the Rhineland. Nevertheless notice had been served on the old peasant republic that its place would be taken over by the new forces of the growing nation states. The headquarters of the Society moved soon after the civil war from Visby to Lübeck, where it was developed into the famous German Hanseatic League. From 1299 the Society's seal was no longer used in Visby, and the Gotlanders' ancient trading posts, including the most renowned of all at Novgorod, were sold to their competitors. Gotland, no longer Queen of the Baltic, was becoming a pawn in the power struggle between the new kingdoms of Northern Europe.

27 JULY 1361

The second half of the fourteenth century was marked in the North by a feud between Denmark and Sweden, the latter being usually supported by the Hansa. In particular the Danish King Valdemar Atterdag exacted a high price from Hansa towns in his territory for the continuance of their trading privileges. As Visby was a rich Hansa town well worth squeezing and—probably a more important consideration at the time —as Gotland was a Swedish possession well placed to cover the south-east coast of mainland Sweden and well suited to act as a useful pawn in any diplomatic wrangles, the island became disastrously involved in his plans. Valdemar's invasion in July 1361 was thus not the sudden swoop of a bloodthirsty pirate king dazzled by the prospect of rich booty, but a move in the power struggle. True, its effect on Gotland was calamitous, but, in spite of earlier exaggerated accounts, Visby was scarcely harmed. In the wider context Valdemar's conquest of Gotland tilted the balance of power in the North towards Denmark and away from Sweden for the next 400 years.

Crossing from Öland, the Danes landed on the south-west coast of Gotland in the middle of July. Easily defeating at Ajmunds the hastily assembled levies of inexperienced peasants, they made for Visby. Unlike the Gotlanders proper the burghers of Visby had had advance intelligence of Valdemar's expedition, and for reasons that are not clear but were probably as base as is traditionally assumed they neither opened their gates to give shelter to the Gotlandic levies as they neared the town nor sallied forth to help them. Prudence overcame whatever valour these calculating merchants possessed, and from their walls they watched the seasoned Danish mercenaries slaughter the last reserves of the Gotlanders.

This terrible battle runs like a blood-red thread through the fabric of the island's later history. How terrible it was became only too clear in 1928–30 when several mass graves of nearly 1,200 of the 2,000 or so victims were systematically examined. In one grave less than half those buried had been of military age (20 to 55 years). There were skeletons of cripples, invalids and even women among the grim finds. Most had ghastly wounds, many several, and some so many that their pitiful remains are shameful to contemplate as evidence of human savagery. There are macabre collections of bones and weapons in Gotlands Fornsal, the Historical Museum in Stockholm and the National Museum in Copenhagen; but, in fact, once the shock and the pity have passed, one realises that these finds are of great importance in the history of armour.

Valdemar next accepted the surrender of Visby. Part of the walls were broken down so that, in the traditional manner of medieval conquerors, he could ride through the breach into the city in a symbolic assertion of authority. A short stretch of the south-eastern wall, of different construction from the rest and with thirteen crenellations allegedly representing the thirteen knights abreast who rode through it in the train of the Danish king, is to this day pointed out as 'Valdemar's Breach'. He then exacted from the wealthy burghers a rich tribute which legend has undoubtedly exaggerated. Visby could well afford what she was made to pay (and, in any case, included in the ransom was a proportion of the goods of other Hansa towns then stored there). Neither her influence, reinforced by the agreement with Valdemar, nor her wealth were seriously damaged, whereas the Gotlanders had lost many men and much wealth. The difference in the power of the two communities, already growing since the quarrel of 1288, was now enormous. Visby continued to flourish while the country decayed. To that extent the inactive, not to say cowardly, policy of the Visby merchants succeeded brilliantly.

It was far different in the countryside. Since that day until the present century no new church was built in the formerly prosperous hamlets, and many then under construction were never finished. 'The farms are burnt, the sorrowing people fall by the sword.' So reads, in a rather free translation, the Latin inscription on an arch in Fide Church over a fresco of Christ as the Man of Sorrows: and the first letters of the Latin words spell out the year 1361. A few hundred yards east of Visby's wall, by the site of the old Franciscan monastery, a Celtic cross marks the graves of those who fell fighting Valdemar's men. The Latin inscription on it reads: 'In the year of Our Lord 1361 on 27 July before the gates of Visby the Gotlanders here buried fell at the hands of the Danes. "Pray for them".'

'Before the gates of Visby'—how graphically the terse, reproachful phrase describes the scene! But the cross commemorates more than the death of these poor brave people. It also marks the end of Gotland's glory.

6   FROM DANISH RULE TO MODERN TIMES

UNDER DENMARK

AFTER appointing Danish bailiffs to control the country-side, and collecting his booty from Visby, King Valdemar sailed away never to return. From 1361 to 1645, when it was returned to Sweden by the Peace of Bromsebro, Gotland was formally under the Danish crown. But it was only in the last 100 or so years of this period that the Danes asserted their rule —and this through governors generally little better than the glorified pirates, Danish and other, who had plagued the island for the previous 200 years.

The Danish rule started badly. One of Valdemar's ships full of booty, including the fabled red carbuncles from the west windows of St Nicholas' Church in Visby, was wrecked near the Charles Islands. Legend has it that in suitable conditions (which seem very seldom to have occurred in modern times!) the gleaming semi-precious stones may be seen beneath the sea. The countryside was ruined and the city shaken, but neither was cowed. The yeomen of Gotland kicked out the Danish bailiffs in 1362, while Visby showed some mettle by joining its Hansa colleagues in their fight against Valdemar for the control of the very lucrative traffic from the North Sea to the Baltic through the Sound (Öresund) between Denmark and South Sweden. Two years later, at the 'Hansa Day' celebrations in Lübeck on 25 May 1364, Visby was represented not as a Danish vassal but as a proud member of the 'German Hansa'.

A few years later the Hansa towns again challenged Valdemar for control of the Sound. In fact they won it, but in their agreement with the Danish king did not bother to have Visby's equivocal status changed. Neither Visby nor Gotland mattered very much any more. They were useful from time to time and, at least at the beginning of this period, worth the occasional raid, but they were not important politically.

For most of the next three centuries Gotland was in a poor way. Its living standards now for the first time for centuries were reduced to about the same level as the rest of Northern Europe. Compared with its previous affluence, this was poverty. At the same time the Gotlanders had lost their independence in a disastrous battle. It is not surprising that the double shock has traditionally led to sentimental longings for the Golden Age. Visby remained an important and prosperous port for much of the period, but was in decline towards its end. That it was worth plundering three times in 4 years at the end of the fourteenth century by the fanatical Vitalian Brothers speaks for itself. So also does the new work done to the churches in Visby at this time, particularly when set against the complete cessation of building in the countryside.

The Brothers, a well organised band of pirates, originally from Mecklenberg in North Germany, became the scourge of the south-eastern Baltic towards the end of the century. 'God's Friends and all Men's Enemies', as they arrogantly styled themselves, they based themselves on Visby while engaged on providing supplies (or 'victualling', hence the name) for Stockholm when it was under attack from the Danes. After some years of high-handed depredation under Albert of Mecklenberg they were expelled from Visby in 1398 by the powerful Teutonic Knights from the Baltic states to the east. For a while Visby enjoyed order and good government, but was then sold to King Eric of Pomerania by the Knights in 1408. This event is of some importance because it was Eric who built the famous, but now vanished, fortress of Visborg at the south-western corner of the

Page 71 (*above*) Uggarde Rojr—the biggest of about 400 'Big Cairns' from the Bronze Age on Gotland; (*below*) low, walled graves at Trullhalsar, one of nearly 1,000 sites from the Iron Age with over 25,000 graves in all

(*left*) Bronze Age ship-grave at Gannarve on the west coast of Gotland. The ponies—the ancient local 'russ'—give an idea of the size of the monument; (*below*) Trojeborg maze near Visby, an intriguing relic of unknown age and purpose, but probably connected with a medieval game

city walls. It was to Visborg that Eric retreated, when expelled from his kingdom, to spend the last 10 years of his rule there in debauchery enlivened by piracy and the frequent onslaughts of his many enemies. In one attack Visby was set on fire and saved from total destruction only by Divine Intervention.

In 1449, however, the Danes reasserted their sovereignty over Gotland, captured Visby and installed in Visborg the first of a long line of generally undistinguished governors. Paying scant allegiance to their king in Copenhagen, they concentrated on exploiting their independent position for their own considerable profit.

The first three governors were all members of the powerful Axelsson Tott family, who treated Gotland as their own great feudal estate. His two elder brothers soon dying of plague, the youngest brother, Ivar Axelsson Tott, took over what had now for practical purposes become a family fief and ruled it with imagination and authority. He was a manifestation in Northern Europe of the well known medieval barons and powerful vassals who sought elsewhere to carve out their own kingdoms from their sovereign's land. He had important strongholds in Sweden, Finland and the Baltic states, vast family estates in Denmark and royal connections. No wonder that from his strategically well sited base on Gotland he challenged the king of Sweden and dreamt of a new Baltic Empire with Visby as its capital. But he extended himself too far and his plans miscarried.

THE DESTRUCTION OF VISBY

In the first decades of the sixteenth century another ambitious governor of Gotland, Sören Norrby, again involved the island —this time disastrously—in the continuing triangular conflict between Sweden, Denmark and the Hansa, with the regular opportunities it provided for piracy and lucrative raiding. Under Norrby's active, if unscrupulous, rule both Gotland and

E

Visby regained some measure of their old prosperity. He struck his own coins regardless of his legal status as a servant of the king of Denmark. He appears in fact to have been popular and the accepted leader of the Gotlanders, whose support, for example, when the Swedish king unsuccessfully sought to drive him out of the island, undoubtedly prolonged his reign.

But he had antagonised too many powerful opponents. In the summer of 1525 this 'last of the Knights' crossed to Southern Sweden, then a Danish province, to try to raise the disaffected peasants against their king and thus forestall the attack he had learnt the Danes planned to make on Gotland. Unfortunately the men of Lübeck were in league with the Danes. Sailing across the Baltic to join them they discovered that Norrby was away and Gotland undefended. They attacked Visby on Whit Sunday morning, 13 May 1525, while most of the inhabitants were at Divine Service, broke through the wall at its north-west corner and stormed the city. St Mary's, the German community's own place of worship, was not attacked, but many of the splendid medieval churches were destroyed or damaged, and with them other important buildings of old Visby.

Danish rule was now reimposed in earnest by a series of governors of interest only for their rapacity. A gloomy era of arbitrary over-taxation and dull stagnation was ushered in; and both Gotland and Visby reached the nadir of their fortunes. It is nevertheless worth noting that under one of them, Rosenkrantz, the Reformation was peacefully introduced to the island in 1537, a fine memorial in Visby Cathedral being the governor's reward. About the only other matter worth noting from these uninspiring times is the biggest sea disaster that ever happened in the Baltic, also commemorated by a memorial in Visby Cathedral to the commander of the forces involved, Vice-Admiral Thinnapfel. What happened was that in July 1566 the combined fleets of Denmark and Lübeck had come to a point off Visby to bury at sea the victims of a battle off Öland

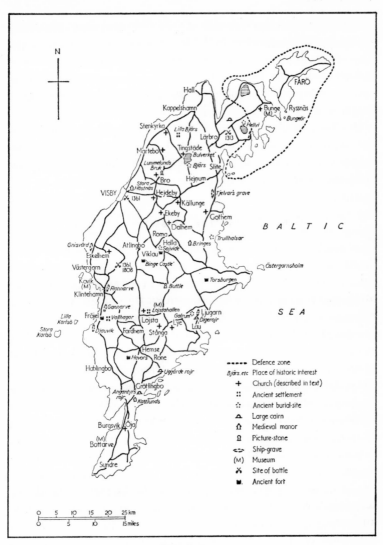

N

Hall

Kappelshamn

Stenkyrka
Lilla Bjärs
Lärbro
1313

Martebo
Tingstäde
Bulverket
Bjärs
Slite
Lummelunds
Bruk
Bro
Hejnum

Stora
Hästnäs
Hejdeby
Källunge
Tjelvar's grave

VISBY
1361

Ekeby
Dalhem
Gothem

Roma
Halla
Sojvide
Trullhalsar
Bringes

Gnisvärd
Atlingbo

Eskelhem
Viklau
Binge Castle
1361
1808

Västergarn
Östergarnsholm

Kovik
(M)
Rannarve
Klintehamn
B. Buttle
Torsburgen

Gannarve
(M)
Lojstahallen
S E A

Lilla
Karlsö
Fröjel
Vallhagar
Galrum
Ljugarn
Digerojr
Stora
Karlsö
Lojsta
Lye
Lau
Djauvik
Fardhem
Stånga

Hemse
Havors
Rone
Hablingbo
Uggarde rojr

Grötlingbo
Angantyrs
rojr
Kattlunds

Burgsvik
Oja
(M)
Bottarve

Sundre

B A L T I C

FÅRÖ
Bunge
Ryssnäs
(M)
Bungeör
Hellvi

- - - - -	Defence zone
Bjärs.etc	Place of historic interest
+	Church (described in text)
::	Ancient settlement
∴	Ancient burial-site
△	Large cairn
⌂	Medieval manor
Ω	Picture-stone
⟷	Ship-grave
(M)	Museum
⚔	Site of battle
⛫	Ancient fort

0 5 10 15 20 25 km
0   5   10   15 miles

Historical map

with the Swedes. A sudden storm blew up and drove the ships
ashore, wrecking them with the loss of from 6,000 to 8,000 men.
Twelve of the warships were Danish and three came from
Lübeck. In 1960 divers investigated the wrecks and found
various personal belongings, including a silver spoon belonging
to the vice-admiral.

In 1618 the Danish king abolished the ancient assemblies of
free men (*ting*) which had existed since Viking times. This
action was symbolic of the depression in Gotland during the
last years of Danish suzerainty.

THREE CENTURIES OF SWEDISH RULE

In 1645, when Sweden and Denmark concluded the Peace of
Bromsebro, Gotland, rather as an afterthought—a final bar-
gaining counter to ensure agreement—was given back to
Sweden. There was little enthusiasm for the change. Gotlanders
who did not wish to live under a new king were allowed a year
to settle their affairs and leave the island. The Swedes were seen
as interfering foreigners, resented for their efficiency and their
subordination to the central bureaucracy in Stockholm, with
its newfangled theories of modernisation and industrial development. Lawless and remote from the control of Copenhagen as
Gotland was under the Danes, there was then at any rate a form
of rough independence, with pickings for all, especially the
strong. The ideas and forms of government the Swedes introduced were inimical to the old order and as such disliked.

The country was poor, but, as often in the story of Gotland,
certainly not as poor as later apologists have maintained. Their
understandable exaggeration reflects the discontent the islanders
felt at enforced changes as much as their comparative poverty.
Change in fact came slowly but decisively. In particular the
establishment in 1653 of the individual farm in place of the old
commune as the unit of taxation had a profound effect. It broke
up a pattern of land tenure and of country life that had lasted for

1,000 years and given Gotland much of its unique character. Similarly the imposition of excise taxes was resented by traditional free-traders, even though the new and closer connection with Sweden led to a general increase in trade, especially with Stockholm—a pattern which has persisted. Taxes on 'fat goods' —tallow and butter, for example—which could profitably be sold abroad were specially resented. So was the tax on the train oil produced by the important local seal fisheries at a time when the expansion of whaling round Spitzbergen and Greenland provided hard competition anyhow, and the comparatively large payments that had to be made to the priest and the judge. Finally the fact that nearly three-quarters of the annual income the crown derived from Gotland in the middle of the seventeenth century (Gotland being a royal domain) went to support the reputedly profligate Queen Christina in luxurious exile in Rome did nothing to lessen complaints.

In accordance with contemporary economic theories on the division of labour and the exploitation of a country's native resources, charters were given to Swedish entrepreneurs to develop Gotland so that it could make an appropriate contribution to the well-being of the Motherland. Factories were opened (one made clothes) and foundries established, but they received scant support from either the Gotlanders or the Visby merchants. Except for Lummelunds foundry, all soon became bankrupt. To some extent this reflected a general depression which hit Visby so hard that there was talk of transferring its status and privileges as a city to Slite on the north-east coast. It had an excellent harbour, a shipyard had been established there and it was becoming increasingly important as the centre of the flourishing new lime-burning industry. But trade generally was sluggish, reflecting the unsettled times, in which in fact several raids were made on Gotland by Sweden's enemies. Indeed from 1676 to 1679 the Danes again ruled Gotland briefly and, being forced to cede it by the Treaty of Lund, blew up Visborg Castle before they left.

ROADS AND POTATOES

During the eighteenth century conditions improved. Lime-burning boomed, although it produced a new, and socially divisive phenomenon on the previously class-less Gotland by establishing a sharp cleavage between rich kiln-owner and poor hired hand working for him. Agriculture, too, picked up, its recovery being helped by the forceful and enlightened policies of two governors in particular—Grönhagen (died 1738) and von Segebaden (1765–87). The latter, against strong opposition from conservative farmers, introduced potatoes to the island; and laid the foundation of a system of modern roads, particularly in the northern part of the country.

In consequence the island in general and Visby in particular became prosperous once more, though there were several important differences between this period and the Golden Age. The first was that most of the trade was now concentrated in the hands of a few big merchants, among whom the families of Donner, Dubbe and Lythberg were most prominent. The remains of one of the Donner family's estates may be seen at Hallfreda about 10 miles south-east of Visby; and an observation tower built by Dubbe on his estate, though now ruined, still stands at Rosendal near by. A significant indication of the extent of such merchants' interests is the fact that, in 1785, the firm of Donner was in correspondence with seventy different foreign towns, and had several correspondents in many of them. Moreover, the high returns from trade by neutral vessels in the American War of Independence helped appreciably to swell profits already growing from the general upsurge of prosperity.

The second factor which differentiated the pattern of Gotlandic commence at this period from that of the great years of the thirteenth century was that the country ports, as in the late Viking Age, again accounted for most of the island's trade. Visby was obviously doing well, but other ports, in particular

Burgsvik and Klintehamn, were handling as many ships. In fact it was not until the middle of the nineteenth century, with the advent of steamships and the first developments of Visby's modern harbour, together with the growth of its importance as the island's capital, that these smaller ports ceased to play a major role. Several of them have recently become important again for specialised trade (see Chapter 7).

A BLOODLESS RUSSIAN INVASION

Napoleon's grandiose scheme of closing all the ports of Europe to English trade by his Continental blockade brought the British Navy into the Baltic to prevent its application there and to harass the Russians, who were allied with the French. In 1808 Swedish warships were co-operating with British ships to watch the Franco-Danish fleet and to contain the Russians. If, as was to be expected, the Russians retaliated, Gotland, as the eastern outpost of the Swedish realm, would clearly be in danger. The slight importance the deranged king of Sweden, Gustav IV Adolf, attached to Gotland had been shown by his amazing offer, on 1 July 1806, of the island to the Knights of Malta, recently expelled by Napoleon from their ancient stronghold, in language identical to that used in 1530 by Charles V of Spain when he offered Malta to them. The Knights (who hoped for better things from the Czar) had ignored the Swedish gesture. But the Gotlanders had a firmer grasp on reality than their king and, as the sails of warships crossed their seas and the Russians invaded Finland, got ready to defend themselves.

On 22 April 1808 a Russian force of 2,000 men under Admiral Bodisko landed on the south-east coast at Sles near Grötlingbo. The brave but untrained peasant levies, with primitive weapons, assembled to contest the invaders' advance at the bridge at Ajmunds, between Mästerby and Klintehamn, an ancient strategic keypoint of ill omen; it was here that the Gotlanders in 1361 lost their first battle with the invading Danes. Now, however, the prudent governor persuaded his men to yield to the Russians' superior strength and weapons. A comic opera interlude followed. The Russians marched peacefully into Visby, where the admiral and his officers became the darlings of the city's salons, received as welcome guests rather than victorious invaders.

News of the enemy's landing had been quickly sent to Sweden. The Swedish fleet sailed from Karlskrona to Sandviken on the east coast of Gotland north of the Russians' landing-place, thus crossing their lines of communication. Swedish troops were put ashore and, on 16 May, a tearful Admiral Bodisko capitulated without a fight. The Russians left for home from Slite the next day. Not a man had been killed on either side in this rather charming encounter. Nevertheless the Russian landing was meant seriously and appears to have been part of a long-term plan for advancing Russia's western defences. In spite of his unwarlike behaviour Bodisko had no doubts about the strategic value of Gotland. 'My Monarch,' he said, 'would rather give up all Finland than hand over Gotland, the possession of which in regard to Russia's trade and the control of the Baltic always remains of the greatest importance for Russia'—which makes his behaviour all the more surprising.

The lesson of these events was not lost on the Gotlanders. Moves to improve the island's defences were started almost as soon as the Russians left. They culminated in 1812 in the formation of the Gotland Militia, the first such territorial force in Sweden. A fort on the islet of Enholmen, which covers the approaches to Slite Harbour, was also started; but work on it proceeded slowly and spasmodically.

A BALTIC MALTA

The strategic importance of Gotland also involved the island in the Crimean War in 1854 and 1855. In this little known interlude, overshadowed by the fighting in the Crimea and the Charge of the Light Brigade, a large Anglo-French squadron based itself on Fårösund in the north of the island to contain the Russian Baltic Fleet. On the outbreak of war Sweden and Norway had issued a joint proclamation of neutrality and Gotland, being in an important and exposed position, had its defences strengthened. The Swedish government nevertheless tacitly connived at the stationing of the Allied fleet in its waters. So, on 1 April 1854, the first British ship sailed into Fårösund on reconnaissance. It was followed in the middle of the month by coalers and supply ships, which established large dumps ashore. At the same time the British Vice-Consul from Visby, a local shipping man named Enquist, set up an office on which the British and Swedish flags flew side by side until the Anglo-French forces left for good the following year.

The main fleet arrived soon after these events. The British warships were mainly steamships, or mixed steam and sail, and the French mainly sailing ships; this was the last time warships were under sail on active service in European waters.

For the next two summers ten to twelve Allied men-o'-war with attendant supply ships and Norwegian, Danish, German and Dutch victuallers lay constantly in the Sound. When the main fleet was back from blockading the Russian coast as many as fifty warships were present, and occasionally about seventy. The fleet was commanded by Admiral Sir Charles Napier, flying his flag in HMS *Duke of York*, 128 guns, a four-decker driven by both steam and sail and with a crew of over 1,000 men. The French flagship was the *Cressence* under Admiral Déchênes. Both were berthed at the southern entrance to Fårösund to sea-ward of the islet of Bungeör, where a butchery and galley were set up. A hospital ship, HMS *Belleisle*, lay between Bungeör and Ryssnäs (the southern tip of Fårö), while anchorages for the rest of the fleet were found farther up the Sound to the north. The allied strength fluctuated from 1,500 to 10,000 men.

Napier's instructions were defensive:

. . . to stop all Russian ships met; to keep a close watch on the
Åland Islands against Russian moves; to defend Swedish and
Norwegian territory against Russia; to keep watch on the
fortresses of Sveaborg, Kronstadt, Reval and other Russian
bases; and not to take unjustified risks.

In pursuance of this policy he captured numerous prizes (mainly
Finnish vessels under the Russian flag) and cautiously recon-
noitred several of the main Russian bases. His only offensive
action of note was to attack Sveaborg (Bomarsund) in the Åland
Islands on 9–10 August 1855, when both sides expended a lot of
ammunition with little result. On the other hand, comparatively
inglorious though its role may seem, this force did effectively
nullify the Russian Navy.

It is pleasant to record that relations between the sailors and
the local inhabitants were exceptionally good. The tone was set
by the leading man of the district, a wealthy farmer and general
factotum called Grubb. He obviously enjoyed the society of the
foreign officers and, by all accounts, his fair daughters, Emily
and Mary, enjoyed it even more. An enterprising British parson,
a keen amateur sailor who visited the Fleet on successive summers in his yacht *Pet* and wrote about his travels, was also captivated by these ladies—'the roses of Fårösund', he calls them,
'not doomed to bloom unplucked, nor sing unheard, nor fall to
sleep unserenaded'. Echoes of Malta indeed!

The Swedish troops in the district entered into the spirit of the
occasion. Correspondents for various newspapers were particularly impressed by the gun salutes exchanged by Allied ships and
Swedish batteries or watch-ships. Thousands of hungry sailors
also created a good market for local produce. A sign put up at
this time by some enterprising farmer may still be seen at the
back of the restaurant in Bunge Folk Museum. 'Milk and Butter
every morning,' it reads in an elegant hand. The price of eggs
more than doubled, that of sheep rose over fivefold. While such
good business always helps to gain goodwill, there is no doubt
that the sailors really did deserve credit for their exemplary

behaviour—which was also duly reported by visiting journalists. On Bungeör there is (or was until recently) a notice reflecting British discipline. It reads:

Caution!
Trees and Shrubs are not to be cut or broken,
or any other Damage done on this Island.
H.M.S. 'Belleisle' 16 July, 1855.

A sombre note was brought to this pleasant scene in September 1854, when cholera broke out both in the ships and ashore. Its origin was a matter of dispute. Most probably it came with some Russian prisoners. Luckily the onset of winter's cold checked the disease, but not before about twenty sailors and seventeen Swedish villagers had succumbed to it. Most of the sailors are buried in the 'English Cemetery' near the former sickbay at Ryssnäs, but in Bunge churchyard there is one grave—

Sacred to the memory of John Thomas, Master R.N., of East Looe, Cornwall, died on board H.M.S. 'Archer' at Fårösund, 21st October, 1854, aged 30 years.

A few other traces of this activity remain—a path from the foreshore north of Fårösund town to help men laying out water-pipes to a pond a few hundred yards inland; and the house built, but happily never used, as a cholera isolation hospital in the northern outskirts of the town and still known as the 'French Barracks'.

In 1855 the main body of the fleet, which this year had many more steamships, left in October. Early in 1856 peace was concluded and only one ship, an English three-decker, called briefly in May at the once thronged anchorage. As the local correspondent of *Gotlands Läns Tidningar* put it: 'Now the glorious days in Fårösund have ended. Peace is concluded and the Englishmen have vanished.' Thus ended also an important, though little known, exercise of British sea power.

On two separate occasions later in the century the strains of

Anglo-Russian rivalry were felt on Gotland. There were rumours in 1863 that the British fleet would winter in the Baltic to be ready the next spring, if necessary, once more to contain the Russian fleet, but it never appeared. In March 1885 the local newspaper printed a report that a British squadron had been made ready to sail into the Baltic before the Russian harbours were open. In May a Swedish squadron occupied Fårösund and the coastal artillery there was strengthened. Sweden now had both the means and the determination to maintain her neutrality; but no British ships appeared on this occasion either.

RECOVERY IN THE NINETEENTH CENTURY

Meanwhile the impact of Britain in more productive forms steadily made itself felt as the ideas and machinery of first the Agricultural, and then the Industrial, Revolution, reached Gotland. Their effect is discussed in more detail in appropriate chapters later and only the salient points will be mentioned here.

First there was a false start when, at the beginning of the 1800s, the governor, Jacob Cederström, tried to make Gotland a free port in the hope thereby of recapturing the island's old commercial supremacy in the Baltic. But the pattern of both trade and politics had changed, as we have already seen. Gotland could no longer claim to be anything but an outlying Swedish province, and the range of contemporary ships enabled them to by-pass it. So this nostalgic but unrealistic plan failed.

About the same time the Gotlanders began to try out the new methods of the British Agricultural Revolution, some farmers going to Scotland to study them. The first steamship berthed at Visby in 1829; it had been built by an English firm in Stockholm. The old 'meres' were drained and the new methods of husbandry adopted. As the rest of Sweden, too, grew more prosperous, so did Gotland find there a bigger market for its corn, meat and timber. Industrious and philoprogenitive workers (mainly from the south-central province of Småland) came to the island to increase both its output and its population; hence, from about 1880, there was considerable emigration to the United States. Railways were built, sugar beet introduced, the production of cement started; and all the while Gotland became more integrated into Sweden proper and developed into what it is today—the farm and market-garden of Stockholm and an important source of lime and cement for Swedish industry. In the second half of the nineteenth century the island also put itself on the tourist map, when its milder climate began to attract wealthy invalids from Stockholm.

JUST ANOTHER PART OF SWEDEN?

The process has continued in the present century. Improved communications have reinforced the island's ever closer ties with Stockholm. Indeed, there have been suggestions that Gotland should be incorporated in the Province of Stockholm. Its history in the last 50 odd years of earth-shaking wars and revolutions has been uneventful, although its exposed position has brought it nearer to hostilities than the rest of neutral Sweden.

Gotland's forces were mobilised in 1904 during the Russo-Japanese War and defensive positions strengthened. In World War I the most serious incident, among various infringements of neutrality by the belligerents, occurred in July 1915, when the German minelaying cruiser *Albatross* was driven ashore near Östergarn by Russian cruisers. In World War II the Visby night ferry *Hansa* hit a mine and sank with the loss of some ninety lives in November 1944, and a few damaged aircraft of both sides crashed on Gotland. Towards the end of the war Gotland, like the rest of Sweden, became an asylum for hundreds of refugees from the Baltic states.

So Gotland today is the most easterly and exposed region of Sweden and its only island province. But for these very reasons, and with a proud and distinctive heritage, it is in reality more than 'just another part of Sweden'.

85

7   THE ECONOMIC BACKGROUND

TODAY, as for centuries, farming, forestry and fishing are the main occupations of the Gotlanders. About a third of those in work are thus employed, and many others run smallholdings as a sideline, especially near Visby. Near Visby also are to be found most of the few big estates—reminders of the traditional great farms described in Chapter 4.

FARMING

The average holding is quite small: of 3,200 holdings of more than 2 hectares (5 acres) of arable land in 1971 nearly 3,000 were less than 50 hectares (123 acres). Most farmers own their land, less than a tenth of the total arable area being wholly rented. In the circumstances mixed farming is the rule, with the emphasis on quality and special crops which the island's position and favourable climate encourage. The most fertile land is in the south near Hemse and in the centre round Roma. Elsewhere, especially in the north, the soil is rather barren and rocky. The whole island is subject to drought in the early summer. Farming is highly mechanised: in July 1971 there were 5,138 tractors in use.

Traditional products are still important—wool, mutton, pork and grain (barley, wheat and rye). Since the 1880s rape has also been grown. The sheep was long ago put on Gotland's coat-of-arms and still abounds on the island: of 335,000 sheep in Sweden in the middle of 1972, 86,000 were to be found on Gotland, where the milder winters permit them to live outside the whole year round. There are also about 50,000 cows.

86

The advent of the railways, supplementing the improved connections with Sweden proper which the steamships provided, was of great importance to Gotland's farmers, who began to supply, as they increasingly do, a large proportion of Greater Stockholm's food. Thus dairy produce, processed meat, and fresh and canned vegetables are now produced on Gotland, as are various luxury foods such as asparagus, strawberries and spring chickens. The establishment in 1894 of the sugar-beet refinery at Roma marked another landmark in the agricultural scene. Not only was the sugar an important new crop virtually impervious to drought, but it also had several incidental advantages: the method of cultivation improves the soil for an alternating crop and its by-products—pulp and molasses—are valuable animal feed. Some interesting but so far not particularly successful recent experiments in other lines, such as mink-farming and the production of medicinal herbs, may also be mentioned.

FORESTRY

Forestry is much more important for Gotland than the visitor might imagine. In fact over 40 per cent of the island's total area consists of productive forests, chiefly of pine. The best timber is generally found in the north, though there are some good stands near Öja. The forests have been exploited as far back as records go. They became very important last century when a Scotsman from Perth, Alexander Graham, set up the first steam saw and produced pitprops for the booming coalmines of Britain and the Ruhr. His ruthless methods led the Gotlanders to press for the forests to be preserved, by limiting cutting to the pace of natural regeneration; and a law to enforce this, the first of its kind in Sweden, was passed in 1869. But too much wood had been used for the limekilns well before Graham was born. In any event the remaining forests were saved and still make an important contribution to both the island's economy and society, since about 90 per cent are owned by the farmers themselves.

FISHING

For several thousand years fishing from Gotland meant catching seals. Archaeological evidence shows that the earliest men depended on seals for most of their necessities—for implements and clothes as well as food. Towards the end of the eighteenth century, however, these animals had almost been exterminated and were no longer to be caught in numbers large enough to justify the trouble. Of true fish caught off Gotland the small Baltic herring, the cod and the flounder are the most important. In the last few decades the salmon catch also has been of growing value. Herrvik on the east coast is the most important fishing harbour.

TRADE AND INDUSTRY

Exports

For the last three centuries forest products have been the biggest export item from Gotland, although in recent years their contribution has fallen behind that of cement and food, and vies for third place with that of tourism. At the beginning of the period tar—the real pine-tar, golden and pungent—was important for both medical and technical uses; Gotland's had a particularly good reputation and a ready market in Germany, especially for keeping sheep's fleeces healthy. From the mid-nineteenth century, exports of tar, superseded by other medicaments and preservatives, became less important, pitprops and planks becoming the major items exported. At present pulp wood and battens, with a few planks, comprise the main exports from the forests, which, in 1971, totalled 260,000cu metres.

Stone in various forms has also been a major Gotlandic export for centuries—sandstone from the south, limestone from the north. Many carved sandstone fonts were exported to neighbouring countries in the twelfth and thirteenth centuries. Even

88

Page 89
(*above*) The twelfth-century stone font in Barlingbo Church—an example of a special Gotlandic art form; (*left*) one of the biggest picture-stones of approximately 300 on Gotland. Now in Bunge Museum it dates from about AD 800

Page 90 (above) Silver loot and gold jewellery from the Viking Age; (*below left*) wind-mill on the cliff south of Visby; (*right*) Gnisvärd, on the west coast, one of Gotland's many small harbours

before then and right up to the present day whetstones and grindstones from the same fine-textured deposits were regularly sold abroad, especially in the second half of the nineteenth century. At the time of writing a major customer for them is Castro's Cuba, where they sharpen the knives of workers in the sugar fields. From the sixteenth century sandstone has been sent from Gotland to build some of the finest buildings in Denmark and Sweden—Elsinore Castle (where Hamlet lived), the Royal Palace at Stockholm and Drottningholm Palace, for example. When necessary for repairs, more stone is exported, as in 1901, when 50,000cu ft went to the Palace at Stockholm. Concurrently the old skill in stone carving which earlier produced so many notable fonts was revived and applied to ornamental masonry— altars, decorated windows, memorial tablets and so forth—in which there was a steady trade, as there was, and is, in special stone such as 'Hoburgs Marble'.

Limestone as an article of commerce is first mentioned in 1570. Thenceforth it becomes increasingly important both in its natural state and burnt as lime for mortar. When Linnaeus visited Gotland in 1741, he was impressed by the amount of lime produced and describes a particularly vast kiln at Kappelshamn '4 fathoms high and 2½ fathoms broad'. In fact at the end of the century about 18,000 tons of lime were exported each year. The industrial expansion of Europe in the nineteenth century led to further increases in the demand for both burnt lime for mortar for the new buildings springing up everywhere and limestone for the recently discovered processes of smelting iron ore and making wood pulp, in both of which much limestone is used. Since the first cement works were opened in 1888 at Visby, to be followed by others, notably Cementa AB at Slite (formerly Skånska Cement), exports of cement have steadily grown in importance and amounted to 800,000 tonnes (780,000 tons) in 1971. Limestone in various forms has traditionally accounted for about a third of Gotland's exports. In 1972 the company concerned, Gotlands Förenade Kalkbrott AB, expects to export 1·2 million

F

tonnes, over half of this going to Germany, Finland, Denmark and Norway.

In the last few decades exports of food have steadily increased. Between the wars the amount of basic foods—meat, sugar, wheat—sent abroad grew steadily. In the 1930s grain was particularly important, accounting for about half the total value of exports and much of it going to England. Limestone at this time contributed only a fifth of the exports in value. Since the growth in both size and wealth of Greater Stockholm in the last 20 or so years, luxury foods have taken an ever larger share of exports; and Gotland is well on the way to becoming the larder of Stockholm. This dependence illustrates the change in the pattern of Gotlandic trade in the last 100 odd years from a world to a mainly Swedish market.

Imports

Up to the Middle Ages most of what Gotland imported was re-exported in the flourishing entrepôt trade of which the island was then the centre. Retained imports consisted of special food —salt, malt, spices—and luxury items such as precious metals or rich textiles. Throughout this period there was a big export surplus. What happened in the confused years of Danish rule is uncertain and there are few statistics to enlighten us.

In the seventeenth and eighteenth centuries imports and exports were generally in balance, though food had sometimes to be imported in bad years to feed the growing population. The expansion of agriculture and industry in the nineteenth century created a demand for machinery and fuel that could be satisfied only by rising imports, which tended to overtake exports. In the 1930s over half Gotland's imports consisted of coal and coke, while about a third was fertiliser, and the balance machinery, salt, mineral oils and a few luxury items. This pattern has continued, except that the imported fuel now consists of petroleum products, not coal and coke, nearly 280,000 metric tons of fuel oil being imported in 1971.

Industry

The production of cement is now the main industry of Gotland. The Cementa AB works, opened in 1965, has an annual capacity of 1·2 million tonnes (1·17 million tons) and is the biggest in Sweden. The output of limestone, mainly for use in the paper-pulp industry in North Sweden, has also grown in recent years as improved facilities have come into use at Kappelshamn. The opening in 1956 of a power transmission line from the mainland encouraged industry, and several new factories have since been set up, the most important being that of the L. M. Ericsson electrical firm in Visby in 1966. There is a growing amount of food-processing, with canning factories at Visby and Klinteby. At Visby also is Sweden's only hemp factory. About a sixth of the 24,000 or so persons employed on Gotland work in the manufacturing industry, compared with about 200 in mining and quarrying and nearly 9,000 in services, transport and construction.

From the twelfth century to the eighteenth there was an industrial zone immediately south of Visby, where various products were made in the interests of self-sufficiency—rigging and spars for ships, soap and lighting oil from seal-blubber, and similar necessities. Several subsequent attempts to run engineering works, however, including one by Alexander Graham, already mentioned, who opened a firm in Visby in 1874, came to grief because there was simply not enough business.

POWER

Being an island, Gotland is windy, and wind was an important source of power for many years. There are the remains of some very fine windmills in various places, the biggest being just south of Visby. In Bunge Folk Museum are others, much older and now rebuilt. Wind power was used to drive machinery of all sorts—for pumping, and in sawmills—not only for grinding corn.

The first steam saw was introduced in May 1855 from Scotland by Alexander Graham, as we have said; and steam thenceforth became an important, and eventually the main, source of power until ousted by electricity. This is thermally generated. Attempts to use the considerable deposits of peat as fuel, however, have not been successful. Nor in view of the flatness and comparative dryness of the island is there enough water power to make electricity, though before the meres were drained there were numerous small installations driving small machines. Wood, then coal, and now oil have successively been the main sources of power. The first electricity generating station on Gotland was set going in Visby in December 1904, and electric street lights were switched on a few days later.

The price of imported fuel made the cost per unit higher than on the mainland, where hydro-electric plants spread the use of cheaper electricity. Hence Gotland lagged behind. In 1954, however, a new form of power transmission, invented by the Swedish firm of ASEA, was used to connect Gotland to the main-land's supplies. This was a high-voltage direct current trans-mission with mercury-arc rectifying valves carrying 20mW from Västervik to north of Visby.

The advantages of dc transmission of electricity have been known since Faraday. For a given basic insulation level a dc line can operate at a higher voltage than an ac. It needs only two conductors, or even one, compared with the three of an ac line, which makes it simpler and cheaper. Dc earth-return currents go through the earth itself, the molten interior providing an excellent conductor (and saving an expensive copper cable). The system, however, was not practical until the technical diffi-culties of converting dc to ac at the end of the transmission-line were solved by ASEA's development of suitable rectifiers. It has since been employed mainly under the sea across the English Channel, in Japan, New Zealand, between Sardinia and Corsica, in California (the Pacific Intertie) and elsewhere.

The capacity of the power line has now been increased to

30mW at a cable voltage of 150kV, on the substitution in May 1967 of thyristor valves for the previous mercury-arc rectifiers— the first time this technique was used for normal hvdc transmission.

Concurrently, a very modern thermal power station came into operation at Slite, with a capacity of 34mW in 1966, subsequently increased to 50mW, with four ancillary stations producing 12mW, each remotely controlled from the main station. As a result Gotland, though completely electrified, now has ample electricity for its needs and in fact is able, if necessary, to supply some to the mainland.

TOURISM

Considering the importance of Gotland in medieval trade and the many people who must have visited the island, it is surprising there are no accounts of such visits. In the seventeenth and eighteenth centuries Danish savants, notably two botanists, G. Fuirén and O. Sperling, began to notice the island and the great Linnaeus wrote of his important visit in 1741. From about 1800 more interest was shown in Gotland, especially Visby, and a few comments can be traced. In 1808, for example, a visitor from Stockholm records his amazement at the walls of Visby and his annoyance at the damage being done to the ruined churches by those who were carting away their limestone fabric to burn. (It may not have been accident that 2 years later a Royal Decree was issued preserving Visby's ruins.) By 1833 the governor's annual report was referring to the ruins as a source of extra income from tourists.

The Royal Navy paid several visits to Fårösund during this time, but left no literary records. The first steamship to visit the island, the SS *Ellida*, arrived at Visby on 15 June 1829, and for several summers returned with tourists. In June 1826, one of the first tourists to Gotland to record his impressions, Nils Ekdahl, had landed at Burgsvik, inspected Öja Church and been duly

impressed. An unnamed Frenchman, however, quoted in the
Wisby Weckoblad on 4 August 1837, was impressed only by the
fact that he had set foot on Gotland; surprisingly, few of his
compatriots, except sailors from the Anglo-French squadron in
the Crimean War, had done so before, and few have done so
since. 'I am the first Frenchman,' he says, 'in the memory of man
to have visited this island except for a ship-wrecked Captain.'

The success of the *Ellida* led to the foundation in 1835 of a
company that had built at Västervik the first boat specifically
for traffic to Gotland. Appropriately named *Gotland* she was
102ft long and had 40hp engines by the English firm of Samuel
Owen in Stockholm (which had also built the *Ellida*). Amid
jubilation and gun salutes she arrived at Visby on 17 November
1836, but—alas!—had too deep a draught for the harbour and
also proved unreliable. However, other ships—the paddle
steamer *Aktiv*, commissioned in 1841, and the SS *Polhem*—took
up the running. In May 1865 the Gotlands Steamship Company
was founded with the aim of providing a regular service from
Nynäshamn to Visby, which would become particularly important with the eventual completion of the railway from Stockholm
to Nynäshamn (which in fact did not happen until December
1901). The company speedily acquired two ships—the SS
Wisby in 1866, 'built of Swedish iron, fast, and equipped with a
propeller', and the SS *Gotland* in 1868—and has subsequently
handled the regular passenger traffic. Its newest ship, commissioned in November 1972, is the SS *Visby* of 6,000 tons, which
was built at the Mosor yard in Yugoslavia.

From about 1840 onwards, helped by the new ships, there was
a great increase in visitors to the island, which had gained a good
reputation among fashionable doctors in Stockholm, the seal
being set on this recommendation when the Swedish royal
family built a holiday home at Fridhem, south of Visby, in 1866.
The presence of a large Anglo-French squadron in Fårösund in
1854 and 1855 (see Chapter 8) attracted some English visitors, a
few of whom recorded their comments on the island. But in

general and especially when one considers its long and unusual history and its ancient importance, Gotland has been badly served by chroniclers outside Sweden.

In 1889 the influential DBW society of Visby set up a tourist committee which prepared the ground for the still flourishing Gotland Tourist Association (Gotlands Turist Förening). This body has promoted Gotland's interests as a resort since before World War I, campaigned for better communications to, and in, the island, instituted inspections of hotels and lodgings, and produced some useful tourist literature in several languages. Partly no doubt as a result of these efforts nearly 200,000 tourists, including about 20,000 foreigners, have visited Gotland each year recently, contributing on average something over 10 per cent of the island's income. In 1910 there were 10,000 visitors, in 1920 12,000, in 1930 32,000, in 1960 90,000 and in 1972 over 210,000.

PROSPECTS

Gotland's economy is now much stronger than it was in the early 1950s. It has been diversified and modernised. The demand for its main raw materials remains high, the appetite of an increasingly prosperous Stockholm for its food exports apparently remaining insatiable. More and more mainlanders are also getting a taste for the life of the island itself and establishing holiday, or even permanent, homes there. Indeed there is talk of Gotland eventually being incorporated in Greater Stockholm.

These changes are primarily due to the provision of ample power at a competitive price and the steady improvement in communications. But there is also the appeal of an island like Gotland to the inhabitants of crowded cities affluent enough to respond to it. The steady increase in the number of tourists, too, reflects this trend—and now contributes at least 50 million crowns a year to the island's coffers. There is plenty of room for expansion here, as Gotland becomes better known, for only about 12 per cent of visitors are foreigners.

97

GOTLAND

The exodus to mainland Sweden in search of work that was a marked feature of the 1950s has thus been halted. The big cities with their brighter lights, of course, still attract the young—and about a third of Gotland's population is under 25. But in the changed circumstances a move away from the island is a matter of choice rather than of necessity. Moreover, educational and leisure facilities have improved in the last two decades, so the mainland exerts less pull in this respect than it did. There is some movement inside Gotland from the countryside to Visby and Slite, but the population now remains steady instead of decreasing. In short the outlook is reasonably bright.

8   GOVERNMENT

GOTLAND administratively is one county (*län*) of the
twenty-four in Sweden. Unlike the others, however, it
has no county council proper, but a Communal Council
for both Visby and the rest of the island—which, in terms of
geography and population, is good sense. As capital, Visby is
the centre of the administration. The governor lives there and
the central offices are there, including the historically important
County Archives. The Communal Council has sixty members,
who are elected for a term of 3 years. About three-quarters of
its budget is spent on the health services, which, of course, like
education, housing and defence, but to a lesser degree, are also
financed from the central budget of the Ministry of Finance in
Stockholm.

Gotland elects two members to the Swedish Parliament
(*Riksdag*), and these tend to be right wing. In fact the Gotlandic
electorate, of whom nearly 90 per cent cast their votes, gives about
a third of its support to the Centre Party and just over this to the
Social Democrats, whereas in the country at large the Social
Democrats get about a half and the Centre Party less than a
sixth of all votes.

DEFENCE

Gotland, as the Swedish Government points out in successive
Defence Reviews (the latest being as recently as 1972), retains a
special place in the country's defence—a lookout post and an
eastern rampart protecting the important east-central region of

99

the mainland. It is obvious the forces and facilities there are both extensive and active; and their reactions are regularly tested by the exercises the forces of certain nations carry out nearby.

The Commanding General of the Gotland Military Command, with headquarters in Visby, has under him three army units—an armoured unit, an artillery unit and an anti-aircraft unit—and two naval units—the Coastal Artillery at Fårösund and a radio station at Slite—with supporting staff, both administrative and technical. The Air Force detachment—a Fighter Wing at Fårösund—is under the operational control of the air base at Norrköping on the mainland, but the Commanding General decides its ground co-operation role. The civil governor of Gotland is responsible, in close liaison with the Commanding General, for various activities in support of the armed forces— morale, economic and psychological warfare, civil defence. The organisation described above was set up in 1966 and is considered provisional pending the recommendations of a searching investigation into the whole defence structure.

The primary tasks of the above forces, of which only a small cadre are regulars, is training and mobilisation planning. All Swedish men are liable to military service from 18 to 47, starting from 235 to 490 days of basic training, depending on category, and continuing with refresher courses and exercises until the period of liability ends. The number of conscripts undergoing basic training on Gotland varies from month to month and year to year, but there are seldom less than about 2,000 at any time, of whom all but 200 or so come from the mainland. About a fifth of this number take refresher courses on the island each year. In all the Staff reckons about 425,000 training days are spent on basic training annually and 75,000 training days on refresher courses. The Gotlanders themselves, as befits the descendants of the men who formed the first militia in Sweden, have a very good spirit. Both men and women in the age group liable to military service spend much of their spare time at weekend training camps, the women being volunteers.

The economic importance of defence for Gotland has been touched on earlier. The Defence Department employs about 1,350 people (out of about 24,000 in work) whose wages put 45 million crowns into the economy, exclusive of various social contributions the Department makes as their employer. Conscripts' pay and disbursements on their behalf for medical treatment, clothes and so on bring another 15 million crowns, while the costs of training and mobilisation exercises amount to about 23 million.

The Compulsory System

As in the rest of Sweden the educational system on Gotland has been extensively reformed in recent years, with the prime aim of providing equal opportunities for all, regardless of social or economic standing or geographical location. It is progressive, flexible, thorough and comprehensive. There are day nurseries and play schools for the very young and ample opportunities for short, or part-time, courses at any age. Basic education, compulsory since 1842, now starts when the child is 7 and lasts for 9 years in coeducational comprehensive schools, of which there are no less than fifty-five on the island in nine school districts. The large number of schools means that children from even remote homes have not far to travel; and there is a good system of school buses. Practical vocational guidance is given in the eighth year for a total of 3 weeks in at least two occupations. Streaming is introduced in the ninth year, after which most pupils leave.

Nearly a fifth continue their studies at *gymnasium* level—the equivalent of the British 'A' level, or the American High School. Entry to these schools is controlled by the official policy of gearing accommodation to the estimated demand for trained manpower in different occupations. Courses are of 2 or 3 years' duration and cover technical, theoretical and general subjects— building, agriculture, forestry, commerce, economics, the humanities, social studies, languages and so on. A fine new High School, the Säve School, so named in memory of the two famous Gotland teachers of this name in the nineteenth century, was opened in Visby in 1971 and has 1,500 pupils in the 1972–3 school year. Three other schools of this level—Klinte High School, the School of Agriculture and Agricultural Economics at Lövsta, near Roma, and the School of Forestry at Hejde, near Klintehamn—have a further 200 pupils. About 18 per cent of high school pupils from Gotland go on to university in Sweden proper.

Vocational and Leisure Facilities

There are also comprehensive arrangements for vocational training, continuation courses and leisure pursuits, both full-time and part-time. There is a residential Folk High School at Hemse providing mainly general courses of several months. Classes of all sorts—hobbies, music, drama, languages, technical and professional subjects—up to University Extension level are held throughout the island. In fact, at present there are no less than 1,500 such study circles with 15,000 members (some taking more than one course). There is a special series of vocational training classes organised by the Education Department in collaboration with the Ministry of Labour and related to the demands of the labour market; a new centre for these studies with room for 300 pupils was opened in Visby in 1973. Nursery schools are run jointly by the Departments of Education and Social Affairs.

In the 1973 financial year there were about 1,000 full-time or part-time teachers and officials catering for some 9,000 pupils at a cost of 72 million crowns, of which the central government paid half.

For a population of only 54,000, the above is an impressive performance—and in keeping with the concern for their community and almost Scottish regard for education the canny Gotlanders have long shown.

HEALTH AND SOCIAL SERVICES

Gotland has a comprehensive, and largely free, public health system. There is a big hospital in Visby and smaller ones in Visby, Fårösund and Follingbo. There are also nursing homes in the above towns and at Hemse and Lärbro. There are Health Service doctors and dentists in nine districts, which also have medical and dental clinics; and several doctors and dentists in private practice in Visby and elsewhere. These are supported by the State-run chemist shops (*apotek*) in the main areas, which provide medicines in standardised and economical packings. It is worth noting that dental treatment is free up to the age of 16. There is a 25 per cent reduction between 17 and 19 and there-after in principle the real cost has to be paid—an arrangement which has a most beneficial effect on the diet of the young and their teeth!

Sweden has long been considered a model, to some an extreme example, of the Welfare State, caring solicitously for its citizens 'from womb to tomb'. Gotland obviously shares in this sytem. The first thing that strikes one is that it is directed towards the individual, especially the child, legitimate or illegitimate. For example, if a child's parent or parents die, the child is entitled to a pension of several pounds a week. Housing is subsidised—on Gotland specifically the Cementa AB firm at Slite has a cheap housing scheme for its workers—and so is higher education. In fact, though the Swedes, certainly up to the age of 16 when the state family allowance stops, are very well cared for by the provision of all sorts of free or cut-price services and generous cash payments, more of the social security benefits are subse-quently made as loans from the State on easy terms than is often realised. A further point is that there is a very comprehensive system of job retraining. Indeed the various Departments in this general field—Education, Health, Social Security, Labour—co-operate closely for the benefit of all.

9   COMMUNICATIONS

GOTLAND is well served by modern ferry services, especially in the summer. One main route is from Nynäshamn to Visby and there is one sailing daily in each direction, with two sailings from mid-June to mid-August. The other main route from Oskarshamn to Visby runs at the same frequency. The journey in each case takes 5½hr at night and up to an hour less by day. In the summer season there is a daily sailing each way on the shorter route (just under 4hr) from Västervik to Visby. Visby is also served by a daily ferry from Grankullavik on Öland, as is Klintehamn in the south: this is the shortest (2½hr) and cheapest (25.50 crowns single) of all the ferries from other ports of Sweden. There is also a daily service each way throughout the year from Oskarshamn to Klintehamn. This is also a somewhat shorter journey (4–5½hr, depending on season) than other ferry services but costs the same as they do (38.50 single). All the above ferries carry cars and have sleeping berths. Reduced fares for groups, students, pensioners and round tours are available.

A Finnish company runs a regular summer service from Trävemunde to Slite which enables visitors to get to Gotland direct from north Germany without going through Sweden. The same line continues this service from Slite to Helsinki. Cars are carried and the boat sails every fourth or fifth day. An increasing number of cruise liners call at Visby each summer. In 1972 there were twenty-five such visits, including two by the British India Line's school holiday ship *Nevasa*.

COMMUNICATIONS

The amateur yachtsman, in the summer at any rate, should
have an easy run to Gotland, though it tends to be foggy off the
south coast. Navigational and port facilities are good. The coast
is well marked and well lit, the highest lighthouse (190ft above
sea-level) being at Hoburg. On the small rocky islet of Östergarnsholm off the east coast are the ruins, near the modern light,
of an advanced type of coal-burning lighthouse invented at the
end of the seventeenth century by Cristoffer Polhem, the famous
engineer and a native of Gotland. This type of light subsequently
spread to most of Europe. The first lifeboat station was set up
near Hoburg in 1911, and there are now others on Stora Karlsö
and Götska Sandön, and at Visby and Fårösund. There are
minefields off the east and north coasts—and de-ratting facilities
at Visby and Slite. As a glance at the chart will show, there are
many excellent anchorages and small harbours for yachts.

BY AIR

At the time of writing there are no scheduled services to Gotland
from foreign countries, but a growing number of charter aircraft
on international flights land there. There are from four to seven
flights from Stockholm/Bromma each day, depending on the
time of year and the day of the week: flying time is 50min and
the cost 107 crowns single. There are daily flights from Kalmar,
Norrköping and Ronneby, and at least five flights a week from
Malmö; and in the summer several services each week from
Gothenburg—often convenient for passengers arriving by boat
from England. Linjeflyg, the internal Swedish airline, has useful
reductions for round trips, groups and so forth during the
tourist season.

Air traffic has grown steadily since the first public air service
to Gotland was started in 1925, when a Dornier 'Wal' flying
boat made several trips from Stockholm to Slite. For a few years
afterwards Gotlands Steamship Co operated a Ford tri-motor
seaplane, which landed on Tingstäde Lake. Landplanes took

over in the early 1930s and have subsequently maintained the service from the one airport, a mile north-east of Visby. This handled 220,000 passengers in 1970 compared with 148,000 in 1965.

ROADS

Gotland now has an excellent road network with little traffic outside the few big rowns, and is thus pleasant to drive around. The foundations of the system were laid at the end of the eighteenth century by the then governor, Carl Otto von Segebaden (1765–87). Per head of population Gotland has, after Greater Stockholm, a higher concentration of motor cars than anywhere else in Sweden. In July 1971 there were 15,920 compared with a population at the end of 1970 of 53,835.

The first car, a 2½hp Dürrkop from Germany, was registered in 1905, but car ownership spread slowly. In 1920 there were thirty-four and in 1940 only 1,776. The closure of the railway in 1960 has undoubtedly increased the numbers of cars. The first bus service was started between Tingstäde and Lärbro in 1906. In 1922 a route was opened from Visby to Kappelshamn, and by 1924 buses ran from the main railway stations to the surrounding villages, so that the whole island was effectively served by public transport. In July 1971 there were 101 buses and 956 goods vehicles.

POSTS

Since 1 September 1944 all letter mail from and to Gotland has gone by air, and since 1 December 1962 parcels also—a far cry from the early service on which Linnaeus, who was left behind by a mailboat, comments: '. . . (the boat) . . . was small, frail, ancient and unreliable, like its skipper . . .' The service referred to was set up early in the eighteenth century by local interests to replace an inadequate Danish organisation taken over in 1645 when Sweden regained Gotland. It ran from Visby to Stockholm in the summer and from Klintehamn to Boda, on Öland, in the

Page 107 Industry: (*above*) The small-boat harbour at Slite with the important cement works behind; (*below*) a monument to eighteenth-century prosperity—the ruins of a limekiln near Visby

Page 108
Crafts: (*above*) A Gotlandic potter contributing to the revival of the island's old handicrafts; (*right*) the Old Apothecary's Shop, one of the finest Hansa merchant's houses in Visby, now a handicraft centre

winter, employing a boat used solely for postal traffic. It too
failed to provide a good enough service, and in 1786 the Donner
firm took over the transport of mails on contract, putting a special
yacht on to the service in 1806. Passengers and freight were also
carried, of course, and an idea of the social attitude of the time is
provided by the following excerpts from the list of set charges on
this service:

A Gentleman, Lady or Young Lady with berth in cabin	3 Riksdaler
A small Child of the Upper Class	1 Riksdaler
A Junior Officer	2 Riksdaler
A Serving Woman	1 Riksdaler 40 Kronor
Italians, Comedians, Such Persons and their Wives	2 Riksdaler 24 Kronor
Jews and their Wives	4 Riksdaler
A big Horse	3 Riksdaler 03 Kronor
A big Bag with Bedding or Similar	1 Riksdaler
A big Millstone	3 Riksdaler 32 Kronor
A small Millstone	2 Riksdaler
A Corpse	5 Riksdaler

This service, as mentioned earlier, experimented with steamships, but had to revert to sail in winter. In 1849 a new company,
in which the Swedish Post Office had a one-third share, was
formed to handle mails. It chartered bigger and better boats, to
the satisfaction of all concerned, until propeller-driven steel
ships were introduced in 1860 and a reliable modern system
began.

Several sets of stamps recording various aspects of Gotland
have been issued by the Swedish Post Office, the latest being in
April 1973, when two stamps depicting details from the
'picture-stones' were issued. In September 1971 a booklet with
five stamps commemorating the 'Master Masons of Gotland'
came out. A set showing the City Walls of Visby was issued in
April 1965.

There are now twenty-one post offices on Gotland.

PRESS

Three newspapers are at present published on Gotland. The largest is the moderate *Gotlands Allehanda*, founded in 1872 and now having a daily circulation of about 12,000. *Gotlänningen*, founded in 1884 and with a current circulation of just over 5,000, supports the Centre Party, and *Gotlands Folkblad*—founded 1928, circulation just over 5,000—the Social Democrats. There is one publishing firm, Gotlandskonst, producing books, postcards and maps. In the first part of the nineteenth century several other papers made a brief appearance. The first to be published on Gotland was the *Wisby Tidning* in 1811. It ceased publication in 1825 but reappeared as the *Wisby Argus* up to 1830. These, and several other generally short-lived local journals, are an invaluable source of contemporary history.

TELEPHONES

The public telephone system on Gotland started in September 1882, with fifty members of a telephone association in Visby, using Ericsson instruments. Trials over the railway's system enabled subscribers to be connected to Hemse about 35 miles away—a long way for that time. In 1883 a line was set up connecting Visby to Slite, also a long way for those days.

Plans were made, and a cable manufactured, to link Gotland with mainland Sweden in September 1914, but World War I stopped the work. This would have been the longest underwater telephone cable in the world at that time. The connection was finally made in October 1920. There is also an R/T link now.

The number of subscribers has similarly advanced. At the end of July 1971 there were 22,384 telephones for a population of some 54,000. This figure may be compared with 268 subscribers in 1920 and 5,375 in 1940.

RADIO AND TV

There is a radio station in Visby linked to the Swedish national broadcasting service. It broadcasts two programmes of local news each day for a total, at the time of writing, of 25min. It also has local programmes for schools, and news of the local labour market and sporting events. Until the late 1960s there was also a wired rediffusion system.

Television programmes (625 lines) are relayed from the mainland, though Gotlands Radio has a camera team to cover any local news of national interest.

RAIL

The railway system on Gotland functioned from 15 September 1878 to 1 October 1960. The first part of it, from Visby through Roma to Hemse in the south and about 35 miles long, was inaugurated on the former date by King Oscar I. It had forty-eight coaches, of which forty-two were built by a specialist firm at Landskrona and six by Graham's machine shop, newly opened in Visby, which also subsequently did a lot of maintenance work for the railway.

When the sugar-beet factory was opened at Roma in 1894, the rail network was expanded in this part of the island, and in the next few years spread both north and south, although it was not until 1908 that the southern arm reached Burgsvik. In 1909 the first tender locomotives were put into service. Built by Nydquist & Holm of Trollhättan, they were 2-6-0s with outside cylinders and a twin dome.

Various branch lines, such as those from Tingstäde to Lärbro and from Hablingbo to Klintehamn, were opened somewhat later, the Klintehamn link in fact being the last of all, in 1924. By 1928 most of Gotland was served by a reasonable network, with bus feeder services. But motor transport became too competitive, and in 1948 the State took over the railway system, which was finally wound up in 1960 as quite uneconomic. In many parts of the island the traditional wooden station buildings, painted copper-red, are still a prominent feature, and the line of the track is often discernible.

VISBY

'A VIVID SKETCH OF ANCIENT TROY'

THE comments of the anonymous English traveller 'Sylvanus', in his book published in London in 1847, still apply to Visby, even after allowances are made for his typically Victorian enthusiasm:

> Nothing that can be conceived by the imagination can give the reader an adequate idea of the town of Visby. From the sea it is a vivid sketch of Ancient Troy . . . it is difficult to convey to the Reader the excitement of coming on something so strange, so comparatively unknown as this ancient Scandinavian city.

The sea, the walls, and the towers remain the dominant features of this remarkable town, more reminiscent of Rhodes or Valetta than other cities of Northern Europe. The particular situation of Visby, built on a series of narrow limestone plateaux, facing south-west and protected from the north by both the sheer edges of these outcrops and the city walls, undoubtedly provides a slightly, but significantly, warmer local climate than could reasonably be expected this far north. Also, and one can feel this oneself on a sunny day in June, the narrow walled streets and large buildings reflect and store the heat, adding their contribution to the general effect. As a result walnuts, mulberries, grapes and hops, together with other purely decorative plants from softer climates, can grow in Visby. Linnaeus remarks of his visit in 1741 that the previous very cold winter had killed the walnuts and mulberry trees. Later travellers from the early nineteenth century onwards have to their delighted surprise found them growing again.

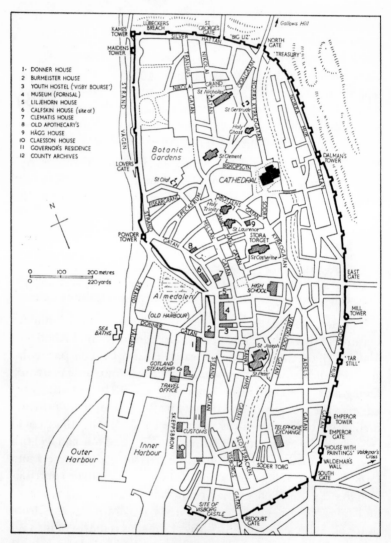

KAMES' TOWER
MAIDENS' TOWER
LÜBECKERS BREACH
ST GEORGES GATE
SILVER HATTAN
'BIG LIZ'
Gallows Hill
NORTH GATE
'TREASURY'

1· DONNER HOUSE
2 BURMEISTER HOUSE
3 YOUTH HOSTEL ('VISBY BOURSE')
4 MUSEUM (FORNSAL)
5 LILJEHORN HOUSE
6 CALFSKIN HOUSE (site of)
7 CLEMATIS HOUSE
8 OLD APOTHECARY'S
9 HÄGG HOUSE
10 CLAESSON HOUSE
11 GOVERNOR'S RESIDENCE
12 COUNTY ARCHIVES

STRAND VAGEN
NIKOLAI GATAN
PANNUS GATAN
NIKOLAI GRAND
St Nicholas
St Gertrude
NORRA MURGATAN
RUTE
DALMAN'S TOWER

Holy Ghost

Botanic Gardens

LOVERS GATE

St Clement
BISKOPSGT
CATHEDRAL

St Olof
FISKARGRAND
SPECKSRUD
BROTHERS CATAN
Holy Trinity
St Laurence
STORA TORGET
SODRA KYRKOGATAN

POWDER TOWER
STRANDGATAN
8
St Catherine
7
6
5
HIGH SCHOOL
EAST GATE

N

Almedalen
(OLD HARBOUR)

4
3
2
VARDKLOVGATAN
MILL TOWER

SEA BATHS

DONNER GATAN

'TAR STILL'

GOTLAND STEAMSHIP Co

St Joseph

St Peter

TRAVEL OFFICE

STRAND VAGEN

SKEPPSBRON

11
CUSTOMS

HANS GATAN

TELEPHONE EXCHANGE

EMPEROR TOWER
EMPEROR GATE

Outer Harbour

Inner Harbour

10
12
VISBÿROS
SLOTTSBACKEN
SÖDER TORG
ADELS GATAN

'HOUSE WITH PAINTINGS'
Valdemar's Cross
VALDEMAR'S WALL
SOUTH GATE

SITE OF VISBORG CASTLE
REDOUBT GATE

0   100   200 metres
0   220 yards

Town plan of Visby

The origin of the town of Visby was for many years wrongly attributed, under the influence of German scholars who exaggerated the importance of the North German towns in early Baltic history, to the inhabitants of the vanished town of 'Vineta' on the River Oder. About AD 800, the account ran, Vineta was destroyed and the survivors settled in Visby, the slight similarity in the names of the two places doubtless being the starting-point for the myth. In fact parts of Visby have been inhabited since the Late Stone Age; and there is now little doubt that, at the time of the supposed settlement from Vineta, an important Gotlandic town was already established there. Its boundaries followed the line of Strandgatan and the curve of streets farther inland, this crescent shape being typical of early Gothic towns. The Germans did play a major role in the city's later development, but they certainly did not found it.

The meaning of the city's name is disputed. It was for long accepted as 'the settlement' (*by*) at the 'sacred place' (*vi*). From the 1940s, however, the explanation has been gaining ground that *vis* is a variant of the Old German *ves*, meaning a marsh. According to this view much of the area of the present town was, until about the twelfth century, marshy—of which there is some proof.

THE CITY WALL

The city wall of Visby comprises an almost intact defensive line some 3,300m long with thirty-seven towers. The oldest building in the complex is the Powder Tower (*Kruttornet*), originally known as the Lamb Tower (after the lamb in Gotland's coat-of-arms of lamb and flag). It was built about 1100 as a fort and harbour-control post before any of the existing wall. The wall as it appears today was built in three main stages, with additions and improvements up to the early eighteenth century. The oldest part is the comparatively low sea wall, constructed in the second half of the twelfth century. Much of it remains between Donnersplats and the Powder Tower, the stretch north of *Lilla Strand-*

porten ('the Little Harbour Gate') in particular giving a good impression of its original appearance. The first land wall was next constructed about 1250, when relations between the burghers of Visby and the rest of Gotland began to deteriorate, and its height was increased, with taller towers, between 1289 and 1300. Changes in the range of weapons led to additions such as the caponiers, or covered forward defences.

Traces of the sea wall can be seen north of the Powder Tower, in particular what was obviously a watergate; that is now known as 'Lovers' Gate' (*Kärleksporten*), largely because the sun setting on the sea behind it makes a good background for romantic photographs. A bit farther on is the famous 'Maiden's Tower' (*Jungfrutornet*), built early in the fifteenth century and owing its reputation to a popular, but historically inaccurate, Swedish romance of the last century. Old and new walls meet at the North-West Gate Tower, where the magnificent sweep of the wall behind its dry moat is well seen. A few yards north of this tower is a low stretch of wall of different construction. This is the 'Lübeckers Breach', where the men of Lübeck broke through in 1525. St George's Gate, the high 'Big Liz' (*Långa Lisa*) and the square and sturdy North Gate continue the defences. Here, round the northeast angle and along the east face, enlightened legislation from the beginning of the nineteenth century has kept the walls uncluttered, so that an impression of their formidable appearance to attackers in the open is still obtained.

Of various buildings on the east wall the remains of the medieval house traditionally known as the 'Treasury', and older than the wall, is of interest. So are the semicircular Mill Tower (*Kvarntornet*) and two other old houses beyond it—the 'Tar Still', so used until well into last century; and the 'House with the Paintings' (*Huset med Målningar*), with fragments of medieval paintings in its upper rooms. Between this house and the South Gate is a section of wall with thirteen crenellations, which is known as 'Valdemar's Wall' and traditionally marks the site of the breach made for the entry of the Danish King Valdemar in

1361. The South Gate itself is more elegant than the others, but beyond it the now fragmentary wall, as it runs down to the shore, is cluttered by trees and buildings. The heavier works here are the ruins of Visborg Castle.

MEDIEVAL BUILDINGS

The lower part of Visby from Donnersplats behind the harbour northwards along Strandgatan to the Storatorget (main square) and the cathedral affords entrancing impressions of what many of us imagine a medieval town was like. From the outside, if one looks with half-closed eyes across the site of the old harbour at Almedalen to the wall, the step-gabled houses and the cathedral, the illusion is almost complete. Scene after scene contributes to it—the half-timbered houses with ochre or white plaster; the red, pointed roofs; the brown projecting woodwork of upper storeys almost meeting across narrow streets; and the road beneath one's feet, usually of stone and often cobbled, in harmony with the nearby walls and old stone buildings. The scale of former days has been preserved—essentially human, but deferring to God, whose predominance is marked by the lofty cathedral. Roses, morning glories and other climbing plants peer out from walled gardens, and trees spread their dappled shade in the winding streets and alleys of this unreal romantic city. As a much-travelled Italian journalist said: 'This is not Sweden. It is a provincial town in central France.' It is easy to see what he meant.

Apart from the dwellings of prosperous merchants, best seen in Strandgatan, the city has about 150 houses, in different states of preservation, of ordinary medieval folk, the Nunnan Café in the Main Square and the *Kronstallet* building in the lane behind *Stadshotellet*, just south of Donnersplats, being the most complete.

Donnerska Huset (Donner House), the present Post Office, a large restrained building whose middle part is medieval, stands near the harbour at the end of Strandgatan. Northwards along Strandgatan one sees on the left the red-brown half-timbered Burmeister House, built by a rich merchant in the seventeenth century and now the headquarters of the Gotland Tourist Association, and on the right some splendid medieval buildings. *Vandrahem* (the Youth Hostel) is a typical step-gabled house of a Hanseatic merchant, with storerooms above the domestic quarters and vaulted cellars below. After that comes the Museum, Gotlands Fornsal, itself built on the site of a medieval house whose cellar still exists; and *Liljehornska Huset* (Liljehorn House), described in 1234 as one of the most imposing houses in Northern Europe. It was, however, extensively altered in the last century. Facing it is a charming little square of elegantly shaped and colourful houses with a fountain and, in season, bright flowers. It is now called Packhusplan, but old maps refer to it as Rolands Square, and it is believed to be the oldest square in the city. Just north of it, along Birgersgränd, once stood the Calfskin House (*Kalvskinnshuset*), a medieval palace of legendary splendour and regal associations. The story goes that when the Gotlanders captured the Swedish King Birger Magnusson in 1313, he was brought to Visby as a prisoner and told he could have as much land for his house as the skin of a calf would cover. As usual in this widespread primitive legend, the hero of the story outwitted his opponents by cutting the skin into very thin strips so that it enclosed a large area. No king ever lived there; for much of its existence it was the seat of the Merchants' Guild, and it ended its days as a wine-bar.

Opposite Packhusplan on the north side of Strandgatan is a charming small merchant's house called *Clematis Huset* (Clematis House), of less forbidding dimensions than other medieval buildings in this street. The next building of note is the large and splendid *Gamla Apoteket* (Old Apothecary's), a magnificent example of a Hansa house, restored in 1929–30 and now in the care of the Swedish Academy. Its high narrow front, with the gable surmounted by long narrow crenellations rather than the usual steps, has no fewer than five large doors for the goods once stored there. It was built at the end of the thirteenth century, and the top floors were converted to domestic use 100 or so years later. It is now the showroom for local handicrafts, particularly jewellery.

Farther back towards the cathedral many medieval features are to be seen; and there are more inside houses with later exteriors. A few buildings here are comparable to, though smaller than, those in Strandgatan, probably the most notable being *Häggska Huset* (Hägg House) in St Lars Gränd, just north of Stortorget. This is a strong square edifice of chunky grey stone, built like a tower, with the typical stepped gables.

LATER BUILDINGS

In and near Visby there are other notable buildings, both large and small, dating from the seventeenth century onwards. On the plateau behind the cathedral and near the cathedral itself there are several narrow lanes of charming old cottages built of rich brown wood, with bright windowboxes and painted shutters and windowframes, or in contrasting timber and plaster: Norra Murgatan and Södra Murgatan, running inside the city wall, are especially worth mentioning in this respect, as is Fiskargränd in the lower town.

Here and there are more imposing buildings with historical associations—Claesson House, on Skeppsbron, a small white and grey seventeenth-century house with ornamental woodwork; the *Länsstyrelsen*, the residence of the governor and County Office; and the *Länsarkivet* (County Archives) near Slottsparken in the southern part of the city. The last two have the low clean lines of the eighteenth century, with an occasional touch of ornament, such as a Royal monogram over the door, and good proportions; and both are coloured in pleasant pastel shades. Some of the nineteenth-century buildings are good examples of styles then prevailing in Sweden. Sveriges Kreditbank in St

Hans Plan, and some of the schools, may be mentioned—solid worthy buildings in grey or red, with rather heavy ornamentation. The fact that these and other structures are not too tall, and the judicious use of pastel shades, contribute greatly to the harmonious diversity of the city's architecture.

Unfortunately, the same cannot be said of the suburbs, though there is a fine modern school to the east and some pleasant ordinary houses. Four prominent windmills stand on the cliff just south of Visby, reminders of the days when the island's plentiful supply of wind was its chief motive power. Houses have encroached on the nearest one, which is very big, a bold contrast of black and white, but the others stand free and are a striking sight. They are called (starting from the town) 'The High One', 'The Low One', 'The Crone' and 'The Scold'.

OTHER SIGHTS

The museum (Gotlands Fornsal) on Strandgatan and the Botanic Gardens in the north of the town are, after the wall itself and such churches as the visitors may choose to inspect, the main sights of Visby. The museum, it goes without saying, has a unique display of Gotlandic material from the dawn of history— Stone Age artefacts, Roman metalware, picture-stones, Arab coins, Viking gold, the grim relics of the 1361 battle and nineteenth-century dolls. It has the largest collection of painted windows in Scandinavia and some fine examples of medieval ecclesiastical art. There is also an interesting nautical collection with model ships, and sections with paintings and prints and everyday objects of old Gotland. It is all very well displayed and guidebooks in English are available. The whole forms a noble complement to the open-air Cultural Historical Museum at Bunge in the north of the island, or the more specialised collections, like that at the Fisheries Museum at Kovik near Klintehamn.

The Botanic Gardens were established in 1855 by the curiously named Club of the Bathing Friends (*De Badande Wännerna*), a group of influential citizens of Visby who joined forces in 1814 to set up a swimming club. This done, they used their talents and money to promote various good works. In its early days the gardens were as much for use as for ornament. In his book published in 1863 the English yachtsman Graves refers to '... the Botanic Gardens, which are very small and are used much for growing white mulberry trees for silk-worms'. The mulberries and silkworms have gone, but the Gardens still benefit from the comparative mildness of the climate of Visby and still grow plants unusual so far north. Apart from such purely botanical matters, they are well worth seeing as a charming spectacle, their collection of roses being delightful.

OUTSKIRTS OF VISBY

The first bluff north of Visby is Galberget (Gallow's Hill). On its more or less flat top fragments of a low wall encircle three tall columns, each of seventeen square limestone blocks, standing a few feet apart. They are the remains of the gallows which stood here from the Middle Ages, and in fact were last used in the 1840s. A little farther on are the remains of one of the enormous limekilns which, especially in the eighteenth century, were so common in the northern part of Gotland and so important commercially.

On the flatter ground below Gallow's Hill is a curious monument called Trojeborg (Troy Castle). This is a roughly circular maze of small stones. Its date and function are unknown. Similar arrangements of stones are known from all over Europe, some probably dating from prehistoric times; and the pattern is found in the decoration of medieval churches. In fact it is most probably the 'pitch' for a game popular in England and the eastern states of America in early Stuart times, similar mazes being found in both countries. Near Hovingham in the North Riding of Yorkshire there still is such a maze called 'The City of Troy'. Shakespeare refers to the game in *A Midsummer Night's Dream*. It had, however, no connection with Homer's Troy, but gets its name from a Welsh word meaning to turn or twist, which obviously the players had to do in a maze.

A mile or so away and some 400yd east of South Gate in a patch of grass is another monument about which all too much is known. That is Valdemar's Cross, a simple Celtic or ring cross with its left arm missing, and a few scratches in the centre where earlier was incised a picture of Christ crucified; it marks the mass grave of the 2,000 Gotlandic peasants killed by the Danes in 1361.

On a happier note and well out of Visby, some 3 miles to the south near Högklint, is situated a charming mid-nineteenth-century villa, with fretted gables, elegant verandah and other features of the style developed at this period for the wooden houses of prosperous Scandinavians. This is Fridhem, built in the 1860s by Princess Eugénie as her summer home. As such, and with the aid of the recently established steamship service, it helped to attract fashionable and wealthy visitors to Gotland. It is now owned by the Swedish YMCA and used as a holiday home and conference centre.

A similar distance to the north-east, past the airport, the forti-fied medieval manor farm of Stora Hästnäs is to be seen. Built about 1300, it is one of the most imposing and about the best preserved of the few great country houses remaining from Got-land's Golden Age.

11   CHURCHES

THE medieval country churches are the glory of Gotland. Of ninety-four in use, ninety-three were built before the end of the fourteenth century. Only two—Fårö and Sproge—have been extensively altered since. The church at Slite was built in the 1950s. Of the sixteen churches in Visby in its heyday, however, only the great cathedral remains intact. Nowhere else is there such a concentration of unspoilt churches from the Middle Ages. The island thus provides a unique architectural museum of the prevailing Baltic Gothic style as distinct from the better known and more ornate Gothic of countries farther south. Indeed one can with justice talk of a Gotlandic style, marked by clean lines, high galleried towers, stepped roofs, deep porches with restrained ornamentation and fine naves—the achievement of local architects and master masons.

If all good architecture is the expression of national life and character, as John Ruskin maintained, these proud buildings bear permanent witness to the piety and prosperity of the Gotlanders before the Danish attack of 1361. As the land decayed thereafter, so the building of churches stopped, as many graphically illustrate. At Källunge, for example, a great work of alteration remains unfinished. Other churches under construction at this time tell the same tale, being often surmounted by obviously inadequate towers. Hablingbo and Martebo are instances. In retrospect this has been our gain: it enables us to see the buildings as they were in the Middle Ages without the later additions that so often elsewhere mar the purity of the original style.

To those who have seen them it is a constant source of amazement that these magnificent buildings are so little known in the world at large, though distinguished Swedish savants have written much about them. Perhaps this book will help arouse the interest these unique churches merit. Notes on the main features of some outstanding churches are given in Appendix A.

THE EARLIEST CHURCHES

The churches we now see are the culmination of a period of about 300 years of building from the conversion of Gotland to Christianity early in the eleventh century to the end of the thirteenth. The first churches, like other Viking buildings, were built of wood—the *stavkyrkor* (plank churches), of which some magnificent examples still exist in Norway. On Gotland no wooden churches remain, though parts of one found at Hemse at the end of the last century have been reconstructed in the National History Museum in Stockholm. At a very early stage sanctuary churches were built in each of the three administrative districts at Tingstäde, Atlingbo and Fardhem. No traces of these remain; but it follows that the present buildings on these sites, as elsewhere, incorporate fragments of earlier churches. Indeed the great expert on Gotland's churches, the late Prof Johnny Roosval, reckoned that no less than 320 separate churches could be identified—an average of more than three on each existing site—and more remains have been found since his time.

ROMANESQUE CHURCHES

The Romanesque style was developed in those countries of Western Europe which had been under Roman rule, and was introduced to others by the spread of Christianity. It is characterised by rough walls without a basement course, relieved externally by buttresses formed as slim pilasters joined at the top by bands of horizontal mouldings or semicircular arches.

Page 125 (above) Smoked flounders are a Gotlandic speciality and are prepared in many small fishing villages; (below) a typical beach on Gotland, sandy, safe and not too crowded

Page 126 Sports and Entertainments: (*above*) A Mystery Play based on the life of the medieval bishop, Petrus de Dacia, is performed every summer in Visby by the Royal Stockholm Opera; (*below*) not Scotland, but Gotland, where the strong man's sport of 'tossing the caber' survives from Viking times

Porches were similarly rounded, with but little decoration, and in Gotland, for reasons of climate and superstition, were positioned on the south front. (From the north came both bad weather and evil spirits.) There was a rectangular nave, a shorter narrower chancel to the east, often with an apse, and at the west end a low square tower with a small steeple on top.

The interiors were adorned with frescoes—'the poor man's bible' in the days of mass illiteracy—many of which remain. This period saw the birth of the great school of Gotlandic master masons whose work reached its zenith in the elaborately carved fronts still standing in most of the island's churches. Their colleagues in wood also produced some magnificent work— crucifixes, Madonnas and intricate reredoses—which may still be seen both in the churches and the collection in Gotlands Fornsal; but they were more subject to foreign influences, notably French.

Churches with typical Romanesque features include Ganthem, Garde, Havdhem, Källunge, Vall and Hall. The last-named is interesting for the combination of Romanesque and Gothic in its original design.

GOTHIC CHURCHES

The great age of church-building on Gotland began about 1250 and ended abruptly about 1400. As both population and wealth increased, bigger and finer churches were built in a Gothic style modified to local taste and local climate—a climate that discourages the external adornments typical farther south. Hence the clean lines of these structures and the disregard of the spectacular outside buttress. These buildings are buttressed inside. The towers have internal supporting arches and receive extra support from their very thick walls, which converge to give more strength. Such a design supports the mighty steeples so typical of Gotland. As Dr Gunnar Svahnström says in his introduction to the invaluable handbook on Gotland's churches: 'The age

H

loved to build towers. It was almost as if there was a competition between the parishes to build the most magnificent.' So the humble old structures were replaced by fine new buildings of great height, with galleries, gargoyles and many-windowed belfries.

The thick walls also facilitated the development of the distinctive portals. At first fairly shallow, the door arch became unusually deep, utilising the full thickness of the wall. As the jambs were brought forward, their larger surface provided the opportunity for enhanced decoration. So we get a typical door with many clustered pilasters, sometimes in contrasting shades of stone. The skilfully carved capitals tend to depict biblical scenes on one side and abstract floral designs on the other. To balance the width of the arch there is often also a large triangular hood-moulding, its apex almost touching the eaves. Religious statuettes, or scenes in high relief, are frequently placed in this moulding or at the point of the arch. The tympanum itself is usually decorated with carved designs. The soffit—the under surface of the arch—has circular crockets (projecting spurs) in harmony with the decoration on the tympanum. Originally the design was often enhanced by being painted, and traces of pigment are still visible on many doors. In short, as Major Heales states in *The Churches of Gotland*: 'The doorways are magnificent and far surpass those in any equal group of parish churches in England.'

As for the wrought-iron door furniture, the same early observer considers that no country in the world could produce its like. Both comments, of course, refer to the high average standard, not to one or two outstanding creations which may well be considered inferior to those found in selected churches elsewhere.

On the south fronts are often found carved stones from the earlier church on the site, of historical interest rather than artistic merit. Occasionally they are arranged systematically in a frieze along the base of the wall or high up near the eaves; but usually they are just built into the wall near a door as a random extension of its decoration. The windows of these Gotlandic churches are undistinguished architecturally, although the steeple windows often have interesting tracery.

The carved stone fonts and the wall-paintings characteristic of the older Romanesque churches remain in most of these buildings; and new frescoes were added. But the great innovation of the Gothic period was the lovely stained glass. The oldest of such work extant (early thirteenth century) is in the north and east windows of the choir at Dalhem. In the next 100 odd years a great deal of beautiful stained glass was used in Gotland's churches; and so much remains that it has been said with justice (by Dr Bengt Söderberg in his excellent little handbook on Gotland) that 'what the medieval glass of France is to Europe, that of Gotland is to Scandinavia'. There are also some excellent wood carvings—roods (crucifixes in the chancel arch), coloured and gilded figures of the Virgin Mary or saints, and reredoses, or altar-screens—continuing the tradition of earlier times. The often spectacular pulpits and pews now to be seen are considerably later additions, introduced after the form of Divine Service was altered by the Reformation.

ARCHITECTS

Little is known of the architects responsible for these superb buildings. The names of several local men have come down from the early thirteenth century—Botvid from Hejnum (where he signed his name in runes), Botvid from Eskelhem and his son, Lafrans Botvidarson (who signed his name on the porch of Hellvi Church). But apart from what might be called signed works, it is not entirely certain which buildings they were responsible for. Hence the experts make attributions (which are not always accepted by other experts) on the basis of stylistic affinities. From a comparative analysis of certain features in various churches by Prof Roosval, one of the most famous

Gotlandic architects has been named 'Egypticus' from his predilection for lotus columns reminiscent of Ancient Egypt. This man—with his school—was responsible for some of the island's finest country churches—Gothem, Grötlingbo, Hablingbo, Stänga, Öja—and much good work in others—the porches at Norrlanda and Lye, for example. He was also a great builder of imposing steeples. In like manner the master masons, whose ranks included the font-carvers described below, have been distinguished on the basis of their characteristic styles and given fictitious names appropriate to their work.

FONTS

The carved stone fonts to be seen in most churches are a Gotlandic speciality. Utilising the excellent sandstone from Burgsvik, a line of master masons produced works of great merit. Fonts were even sent in large numbers to neighbouring lands, where their creators also worked from time to time. Indeed Prof Reuterswärd of Lund University recently estimated that as many as 3,000 were exported. It is in fact probable that much of the inspiration for the early fonts came from work done at Lund Cathedral in South Sweden, on the construction of which foreign craftsmen, including Englishmen from a famous stone-carving school near Winchester, were employed. Certainly there are many Anglo-Norman influences reflected in them. Later, Byzantine influences come to the fore, so much so that some critics speak of a Byzantine-Gotlandic school in the mid-twelfth century. Be that as it may, the visitor has only to look at these works to realise he is seeing something rare and valuable.

The name of only one font-carver is known for certain—Sigraf, active about 1170. His work, to be seen in the fonts at Bro, Lau and Grötlingbo, is curiously stiff and reminiscent of Assyrian bas-reliefs. The name Hegvald is on the font at Etelhem, but there is some dispute as to whether this is the name of the donor rather than the creator of the work; but there is no disagreement about the importance of this remarkable and very early object or that its maker was also responsible for a whole series of powerfully conceived designs that develop consistently in a wild style, with rich interlaced motifs and writhing beasts, similar to late Viking art. His later work, which may be seen at Ganthem, Halla, När and Stånga, among other places, is less violent and more formal.

For the rest the experts have, as with the architects, distinguished between the work of one man, or one atelier, and another on stylistic grounds and have given the unknown craftsmen suitable names. Thus we talk, for example, of 'Master Byzantios', whose work at Öja, Källunge, and elsewhere echoes Byzantine models; 'Anonymus Maiestatis', the unknown 'Master of Majesty', so called from his frequent depiction of Christ in Majesty (at Stenkyrka or Tingstäde, for example); and 'Calcarius', who uses limestone, not sandstone, as his medium.

STAINED GLASS

The importance of the medieval stained glass in Gotland's churches is not merely that it accounts for the major part of all such glass in Scandinavia, but that so much of it is original. The earliest is at Dalhem in the east windows, the style being rather formal with Byzantine overtones. It is German work of about 1225 and has affinities with the glass at Sjonhem. German influences predominated until about 1280, when English and, to a lesser extent, French styles came in.

Some of the finest glass is at Lye, where the virtually complete chancel windows are the biggest piece of medieval stained glass in the North. The style is freer than in most other churches and the colours softer, with a golden effect. The work was probably done by an English craftsman, dubbed by art historians 'The Master of Lye', who was active in Visby between 1320 and 1350. In certain points of style and in specific details the work of this man, which may also be traced in the glass at Alskog and Klinte, has, according to Prof Roosval, affinities with English wall-paintings (notably in the Northamptonshire church of Croughton). Later experts, however, consider the work more German. In any case, it is interesting to record that the British Minister in Stockholm in the 1840s, the Hon Robert Gordon, paid for repairs to these windows (and that at Endre) and for nets to keep the birds off. Barlingbo, Ekeby, Etelhem, Lau, Lojsta and Rone are among other churches with good glass. The latest is at Hejdeby: it has lovely fresh colours, especially a bright blue. Gotlands Fornsal has a good collection of stained glass from various churches.

WALL-PAINTINGS

Few of Gotland's churches are without paintings on their walls. Much of what we see, it is true, has been restored, but with the utmost skill so that the result is an authentic impression of the decoration when it was new. To an English visitor, from a country where bigots destroyed comparable decorations in all except a very few churches, these bright walls are a revelation and a fascinating glimpse of medieval life. As with the churches, there is such a wealth of material that it is difficult to select one for comment rather than another. What follows is therefore a general and historical description with reference to specific works to illustrate points made. But in fact a visit to nearly any of Gotland's many medieval churches is rewarded by the sight of fine wall-paintings. Numerous churches in the southern part of Sweden, it is true, have old frescoes; but Gotland, once again, can boast a larger variety.

The earliest wall-paintings on Gotland are at Garde and Källunge, executed in the Russo-Byzantine style towards the end of the twelfth century by painters from Novgorod. Later work was more dominated by West European and South Swedish influences. There were two main periods of wall-painting in the 400 odd years they span. The first ran from about 1250 to 1350, and the second covered the latter half of the fifteenth century. Before this there is the Russo-Byzantine work mentioned above, and after it various additions up to the early eighteenth century (at Grötlingbo, for example, or Tingstäde). The work from the first major period is narrative and didactic (religious tracts in paint for an illiterate congregation) or purely ornamental (arches at Fide, Lummelunda, Stenkyrka or Vallstena, and ceilings at Grötlingbo or Hejde). It often shows splendid figures from contemporary life, such as the knight at Gothem, together with more humble characters; and the dress and the everyday objects depicted are of great historical interest.

The largest of these compositions is on the north wall of the nave at Vamlingbo, painted soon after 1250. It shows a favourite medieval theme of St Michael, the church's patron saint, weighing a soul, in this case that of Emperor Henry II. Other common themes are scenes from the life of Christ or of the apostles and saints, each usually identified by his accepted attribute—St Luke with an ox, St Olaf with an axe, and so on. At Eskelhem, for instance, the apostles are shown in their symbolic shapes— Matthew a man, Mark a lion, and John an eagle—supporting an elegant circular composition on the ceiling of the nave. On a more mundane level there are many little comic or mischievous details (the dragon-tailed bird swallowing the corbel of an arch in the nave at Stånga; or the gleeful devils making off with quarrelling women at Linde, though this is probably a work from the later period). In most churches one or more crosses can be seen painted on the walls, usually in a circle and often incorporated in a fresco. These are consecration crosses recording the formal 'opening' of the work, or some other important incident in the church's history.

The work of the other major period in the second half of the fifteenth century is marked by a sense of doom and suffering—a reflection of the country's fallen state. The favourite theme in church after church is Christ's Passion, often accompanied by a portrayal of the Last Judgement. Most of these paintings are done in such a uniform style that they are attributed to one artist, 'The Master of the Passion' (*Passions-mästare*), or at least to one school. Among many such works, those at Eskelhem, Hejdeby, Lojsta, Lye, Mästerby, and Öja may be mentioned. A similar theme is found at Bunge, with curiously eastern figures surrounding the cross and with an unusual use of green and brown. In a few churches the work of 'The Master of the Passion' is accompanied by somewhat later pictures in the style of central Sweden: the murals in the chancel at Öja, or the picture of St George and the Dragon on the south wall of the nave at Lojsta, are instances of this.

After about 1520 interest in adorning churches waned. Over the next couple of centuries murals were still executed, but they have nothing of the importance of the earlier ones, though they are frequently elegant and effective. They are often characterised by pleasant blue tones and depict painted drapery—hanging curtains with swags and pelmets, as at Ekeby—or are in the shape of scrolls and similar designs to complement permanent fixtures in the church such as the pulpits or the pews the Reformation brought in.

POST-GOTHIC

In the 300 or so years from the end of the Gothic style on Gotland about 1400 to the end of the eighteenth century work was done in, rather than on, the churches. First, there was the remarkable fifteenth-century revival of wall-paintings, typified by those of 'The Master of the Passion'. Second, the Reformation introduced new forms of worship, notably the sermon, which required different furnishings in the church—a pulpit for the parson and pews for the congregation—and in this period the many painted pulpits and pews were produced. Most of them are excellent examples of contemporary styles.

From the middle of the seventeenth century there was a

fashion for carved and painted sandstone reredoses of considerable interest, and these may be seen in about forty churches,
including Bro, Stenkyrka, Ekeby (repainted in 1802), Gothem,
Stånga, and Öja. But in architectural terms nothing happened
throughout these years.

THE CHURCHES OF VISBY

The ruins of eleven medieval churches may be seen in Visby
today, while one, the cathedral (founded about the middle of
the twelfth century for the German community) is still in use,
towering over the city like a great flagship among smaller vessels.
The foundations of a thirteenth, the long-lost chapel of the
Russian community, were laid bare in 1971 among buildings
to the south of the cathedral, but provide little to see. The remains of two—St George's (S:t Göran), the church of the leper
hospital several hundred yards to the north, and the scant
traces of the conventual church of Solberga about ¼ mile east of
South Gate—lie outside the city wall. According to medieval
sources there were two others in the city—St James's (S:t
Jakob) built by the merchants of Riga somewhere near the
present Holy Trinity, and St Michael's (S:t Mikael) near South
Gate: but no traces of them remain. Visborg Castle also had its
own garrison chapel, which was blown up with it. With at least
sixteen churches, Visby in the Middle Ages had more than any
other town in Sweden.

The earliest fragment of any church still extant is the well
preserved foundations in St Clement's (S:t Clemens) of one of
the first stone churches in the city, dating from the middle of the
twelfth century. There are similar, but smaller, remains inside
St Peter's (S:t Per). The oldest site of Christian worship is
probably in, or near St Peter's, though some authorities claim
that the city's first church (of wood) stood where Holy Trinity
(*den Heliga Trefaldigeten*, Drotten) now stands. The smallest
church is St Gertrude's (S:ta Gertrud), which is also the latest,

having been built by a Danish governor at the end of the fifteenth century. The largest is the sole survivor of these splendid edifices, the present cathedral, St Mary's (Domkyrkan S:ta Maria).

As one would expect from the city's history, the predominant style of Visby's churches owes much to Germany. Both the layout and points of detail of church after church reflect earlier buildings in Germany. There are also some Anglo-Norman influences in details such as doors. One church, St Laurence's (S:t Lars) is basically a standard Russo-Byzantine church added to an earlier Gothic chancel. Nevertheless, from the early thirteenth century and best illustrated by St Clement's, native architects and masons of genius evolved a distinctive Visby style, simpler and bolder than what had been borrowed from abroad. This had a marked influence on the country churches of Gotland.

Even before Lübeck's attack in 1525 caused so much damage, Visby was in decline and her churches with her, but that of the rich German merchants less than others. Apart from the virtually private chapel of St Gertrude's, mentioned above, the consecration of St Catherine's (S:ta Karin) in 1412 marked the end of church-building in the city. Over a century earlier the diversion of resources to build the walls of Visby and country parish churches had in fact signalled that the great days were over. There was not the money either to maintain old, or build new, churches. Then came the Reformation, which closed the three monastic foundations—St Catherine's, the vanished St James's and St Nicholas' (S:t Nikolai)—and hastened the ruin of their churches. In the poverty of the seventeenth and eighteenth centuries the decline continued and was indeed accelerated by the use of these fine buildings as a cheap and convenient source of limestone for mortar, dressed stone, doors, tiles and various fittings. So accepted had this vandalism become that, in 1730, the then governor himself had to be restrained by court action from selling churches for such purposes to raise funds for his new residence.

The tide turned for the better at the end of the eighteenth

century and the beginning of the nineteenth, as the ideas of the Romantic Revival caused men to look with more appreciative eyes on the monuments of their past. In 1810 what remained of the great churches was formally preserved. Private funds again contributed to their upkeep and, in 1863, the first state grant was made for this. Since then they have been in the thorough and expert care of the Swedish Academy of Sciences and, happily, are now safe for ever.

MISCELLANY

ACCOMMODATION AND EXCURSIONS

THE practical good sense and democratic outlook of the
Swedes are evident in the facilities available to the visitor
on Gotland. The island is no 'tourist trap', but a place
where ordinary people from Sweden proper and neighbouring
countries go with their families and find the accommodation
and amusement they want. Like the rest of Sweden, Gotland is
expensive: but one does get value for money and there are various
ways of economising through all-in tours, family reductions,
books of tickets for bus trips or car-parking, and similar strata-
gems. Standards are high and everything is scrupulously clean.
Many people, especially in Visby, speak English and everyone is
invariably helpful. One's hotel, or landlord, or the unflagging
enthusiasm of the Tourist Association's staff can between them
solve most problems.

Accommodation varies from the few large hotels, mainly in
or near Visby, through several dozen pleasant smaller establishments, to youth hostels, camping sites and holiday villages.
There are at the time of writing nine holiday villages and sixteen
officially supervised and graded camping sites, together with
many private houses which take in summer guests. Children
are particularly well catered for, most larger establishments
having playgrounds and playrooms.

The many tours vary from a couple of hours looking round
Visby and half-day excursions to such places as the grotto at
Lummelunda, with its stalagmites and stalactites (unique in
Scandinavia), and the great water-wheel of the old foundry

nearby, to day-long excursions to the south, Stora Karlsö or Fårö. Several firms in Visby supply hire cars at reasonable rates for those wishing to make their own way; and the individualist can use the comprehensive bus system, or become a true Swede and hire a bicycle—or even a horse—for his expeditions. If he wants a quick bird's-eye view of the island, he can bespeak a private aeroplane or a glider. If he comes in his own boat, he can find excellent sailing, with the reassuring choice of no less than eighteen good harbours to tie up in.

SPORTS AND PASTIMES

There are about thirty good sandy beaches on Gotland, the largest being at Tofta, a few miles south of Visby, backed by a large camping site. Snäckgärdsbaden, just north of Visby, which also possesses a camping site, and a large modern hotel with a swimming pool on the cliff, is the most fashionable resort. Ljugarn on the east coast has some good beaches, and one of the oldest boarding-houses on Gotland—a pleasant traditional white wooden building with russet-brown outbuildings. There are more good beaches both north and south of Ljugarn. In fact it is only the north-west coast which lacks them. Many of them have playgrounds for the young, with slides, seesaws and turn-tables; and, for adults, miniature golf courses, or more demanding gymnastic equipment in rings and trampolines. The larger resorts have public tennis courts, as have other towns: there are four at Visby (and covered courts) and six at Slite. There is an indoor swimming bath at Visby, and about fifty public open-air baths in Visby and elsewhere.

The tourist may also indulge in other, more specialised, pursuits. There are some two dozen athletic tracks, thirty odd football pitches and a few handball grounds, not to mention rifle ranges and bowling alleys. The old Gotlandic sports described below are rapidly growing in popularity, but the enterprising visitor is likely to try only *varpa*, a sort of stone quoits, which is (apparently) the simplest. It is played in about sixty different places. There is a golf course at Kronholmen, near Västergarn. Race meetings are held each Sunday in May and August near Visby, with trotting and races for the little Gotlandic *russ*. These ponies may also be hired for riding in the normal way. Sea angling can be arranged at the main harbours and indulged in free anywhere up to 300yd from the shore. There is coarse fishing in the meres.

ANCIENT SPORTS

Three unusual games of ancient origin are still played on Gotland. One is a ball game called *Pärk*, with seven men a side using a small calfskin ball which may be hit with the hands or kicked on a grass pitch of different sizes for juniors and seniors within a maximum area of 60 by 38m. The game is somewhat like the old French *jeu de pelotte*. A second sport is almost identical with the Scottish 'tossing the caber' (*stångstörtning*), though the size of the Gotlandic pole is smaller. The third, and the most popular, also has similarities with another Scottish sport—curling—in that large flat circular stones are used, but they are thrown at a vertical stick, not slid on ice. The stone is a *varpa* and the game, which probably had a military origin, is very old; as mentioned in Chapter 3, *varpa* have been found buried in Iron Age graves. A three-man team throws the *varpa*, usually weighing 4lb (although champions use stones up to 10lb in weight), at a stick 20m away. If the stick is shifted, its exact former position must be hit; and an expert can knock his opponent's stone off a good mark.

These games have grown in popularity since the end of the last century, when enthusiasts started their revival by organising challenges between parishes in the boastful and humorous style favoured in ancient days; and it is fascinating to record that often a team was able to refer to its great victories of hundreds of years earlier when taunting its opponent to a return match. By

1924 interest in old sports had grown sufficiently for the first Gotlandic Games to be held at Stånga. Since 1965 these have been an annual event on the first Sunday in July, and in recent years teams from Scotland have participated.

DIVERSIONS

In the evening during the season there are casinos in Visby's main hotels, which also provide floor shows. There are two night clubs, one of which is in an enormous old windmill. The main hotels also run dinner dances most nights, as do several smaller hotels and restaurants several times a week, both in Visby and elsewhere. Similarly some of the more expensive restaurants have orchestras. There are branches of the Rotary Club in Visby, Hemse and Slite, which welcome foreign members, as do the Inner Wheel, the Lions' Club and the Junior Chamber of Commerce in Visby.

On Midsummer Day there are folk dances and gymnastic displays, with garlanded maypoles, as is still usual throughout Scandinavia. Another spectacle, the operatic Mystery Play (*Ruinspelen*), based on the life of Petrus de Dacia, is performed in Visby at the end of July and the beginning of August.

Information on these many and varied diversions is available in English from Gotlands Tourist Förening, Box 81, 621 01, Visby; the Swedish Tourist Traffic Association, Box 7306 S–10385, Stockholm 7 direct; the Swedish Embassies in London or Washington; the Swedish National Tourist Office, New York; and offices and agents of the Scandinavian Airlines System or the Swedish-America Line.

MUSEUMS

The museum at Visby (Gotlands Fornsal), which has already been described (p 120), is complemented by the open-air Cultural Historical Museum at Bunge, one of the finest in Scandinavia.

GOTLAND

This was created in 1908 by Theodore Erlandsson when the first exhibit, the seventeenth-century farmhouse from Bunge parish, was moved there. It now gives a comprehensive and fascinating glimpse of Gotland's history from the Stone Age to the age preceding the steam, petrol and concrete revolution. The main entrance is a copy of the gate of the vicarage at Riddare in Hejnum parish, an outstanding example of this form of traditional architecture. There is a selection of Stone and Bronze Age burial sites, some excellent picture-stones, and reconstructions of the old self-sufficient farmsteads, with their water- or wind-powered equipment and installations for making tar, alcohol and other necessities.

The museum, which is owned by a private society and maintained by gate money and donations, is open to the public in summer; and to visit it foreigners may enter the Gotland Defence Zone without special permission. It publishes a guide in English.

There is also a Fisheries Museum at the old fishing beach of Korumpu at Kovik, near Klintehamn. At Bottarve, a few miles south of Burgsvik is a small Museum of Traditional Domestic Architecture. Near Lojsta there is a reconstruction of a 'Long House' of the Roman Iron Age on its original foundations. The above sites are marked on the Historical map (p 75).

WINDMILLS

The several hundred windmills in various states of repair on Gotland are of two basic types—circular stone buildings with a rotatable top to which the vanes are attached, and square wooden pole-mills which themselves turn on a fixed solid base. Both types often have long projecting booms, sometimes on a wheel, to facilitate turning into the wind. They vary in size from the big commercial mill, best illustrated by 'Högan' just south of Visby, to quite small contraptions on farms, which normally had several to provide power for different jobs—grinding corn,

Page 143   (above) The old high school in Visby, a good example of a Swedish nineteenth-century public building; (below) the new 'Säve' high school at Visby, opened in 1971, with 1,500 pupils

Page 144 (above) SS *Wisby* 1866, the first boat of the Gotland Steamship Co—length 122ft, beam 25ft; (below) . . . and the latest, SS *Visby* 1972, length 412ft, beam 69ft

sawing, fulling and so on. Some of the best examples of the wooden mills have been moved to Bunge Folk Museum, but others may still be seen as one travels round the island. Some have been lavishly modified as holiday homes. Of others only a few stones or mouldering planks remain to mark their site, on which trees and scrub are encroaching. But the well preserved windmills are certainly worth a closer look.

CASTLES

The 'castles' (*kastaler*) are strong stone towers, sometimes round but usually square, and often placed near a church. These are early medieval passive defences—watch towers and places of refuge in an age of sudden piratical descents. The Powder Tower at Visby in architectural terms is the best example of a square *kastal*; but, in military terms, with the garrison of Visby nearby, it is quite different from square towers in the countryside. These, as noted in the description of Gothem Church, are often a part of a defensive system based on the strong walls of the churchyard, which is often pierced with loopholes. Most of these towers are in the south of the island, one of the best round ones being at Sundre. (The round towers should not be confused with the remains of limekilns, mainly to be seen on the north-west coast at places like Kyllej. The base of a limekiln with its furnace is of quite a different shape from the unencumbered base of a 'castle'. But many of the kilns are also worth looking at.)

FAMOUS GOTLANDERS

Some Gotlanders who left their mark on the island's history have already been mentioned—Botair who built the first church; Strelow, the Vicar of Vall, who wrote the first chronicles of the island; the great merchant families such as Donner and Dubbe; the Säve brothers, who did so much to arouse interest in Gotland's history; and Prof Munthe, who opened men's eyes to its pre-history. A few others are remembered as making their names elsewhere. In the late nineteenth century several Gotlanders achieved fame in England, but none have become prominent in the United States.

If the claims of the partly mythical Petrus de Dacia, first prior of the Monastery of St Nicholas in Visby in the 1280s, are disregarded, the most famous Gotlander is undoubtedly Cristoffer Polhem, the eighteenth-century inventor and engineer. The son of a German immigrant, also an engineer, who ran for a time and not very well the machinery in the industrial area just south of Visby, Polhem is chiefly remembered for the improvements he made to mining equipment as machine supervisor from 1700 to 1716 at the important Stora Kopparberg mine at Falun in Central Sweden. He produced a famous 'hook hoist' employing a new system of power transmission, based on a form of universal joint he had invented. He also pioneered the serious training of mining engineers, made some excellent clocks, invented an ingenious lock still used and devised the superior type of long-burning coal-fired lighthouse already mentioned. There is a statue of him in Visby on a small lawn by Drotten Church, and the Swedish Post Office commemorated him by a special issue of stamps in August 1951.

Another Gotlander with an interest in clocks was Victor Kullberg, who moved to England and became one of the most brilliant and successful horologists of the nineteenth century. He was born in Visby in 1824, and after an apprenticeship with the local firm of Söderberg, moved to London in 1848. There he worked until his death in 1890, the leading clockmaker of his day. His particular contribution to the craft was the invention of the compensated balance, which greatly improved the accuracy of his clocks. He was specially famous for the precision of his chronometers, which won the annual competition at Greenwich Observatory year after year in the 1880s. He first came to prominence when he won a silver medal at the Besançon Exhibition in 1860, and the first prize at Greenwich the following year

146

for the first time. He subsequently won many other medals and prizes.

Axel Herman Hägg, famous in Victorian London by the name of Haig as an artist specialising in medieval themes, has already been mentioned for his work in restoring Visby Cathedral and Dalhem Church. Born in 1835 at Östergarn, the ancestral district of his family, he died in London in 1921. When revisiting Gotland, he produced pictures of its churches and of its medieval aspect as he imagined it. He produced a particularly interesting one of the medieval harbour of Visby, a theme which his more prolific younger brother Jacob, a Swedish Admiral, made particularly his own. Jacob, in his long retirement—he died as recently as 1931—painted many valuable historical pictures.

Another Gotlander to achieve fame in Victorian London was the soprano Matilda Enequist, professionally known as Biondini. Born in Visby in 1833, she died in 1898 in London where she had settled after training in Stockholm and Paris. During her day she was overshadowed by her compatriot, Jenny Lind.

Of the two Säve brothers, the younger, Per Magnus Arvid, the Visby schoolmaster and antiquarian, was less distinguished than his brother Carl, first professor of Nordic Languages at Uppsala; but he was more important for Gotland. His publication in 1856 of a portfolio of some twenty sketches of Gotland and Visby was a major factor in creating interest in the island's monuments at a time when improved communications were beginning to attract visitors. He subsequently concentrated on collecting and publishing old Gotlandic folk tales. He also founded the Gotland Antiquarian Society and the Visby Museum. His work was continued early this century by another schoolmaster, Theodore Erlandsson, who also both recorded old customs and established the Folk Museum at Bunge.

Others, though not all natives of Gotland, may be mentioned for the contribution they made to the country's life while long

resident there. Willy Wohler came to the island at the age of
seven from Germany and subsequently set up the nature reserve
on the Charles Islands; Alexander Graham arrived from Scotland in 1855 as an ambitious young man of 20 and revolution-
ised forestry; and Profs Johnny Roosval, the art historian, and
Nils Lithberg, the archaeologist, identified themselves with
Gotland and added greatly to the general understanding of its
culture. Happily their successors and disciples maintain their
high traditions today.

THE LANGUAGE

Once the official language of the island, Gotlandic is still in
everyday use in the south and on Fårö in virtually its ancient
form; and many Gotlanders in Visby and elsewhere who normally use Swedish are also fluent in Gotlandic. This old tongue
is accordingly still very much alive. The thirteenth-century
Gutalagen and *Gutasaga* are its earliest written expressions, apart
from occasional inscriptions on rune-stones. It has been studied
and recorded intermittently from the first days of Swedish rule,
at first by parish priests, but latterly by better equipped pro-
fessionals, starting with the Säve brothers. From the middle of
the nineteenth century contributions in Gotlandic have appeared
in local newspapers, and there has been a considerable amount
of poetry written in it up to the present day. This bardic tradition is responsible for the fact that some of the most famous
Swedish hymns were composed by Gotlanders—just as the
Welsh have contributed much to English music. A Gotlandic-
Swedish dictionary was produced between 1918 and 1945.

The old language sounds harsh and primitive. As a famous
Swedish actor said: 'It has a singular smack of blood and
heathendom.' It uses many gutturals and broad diphthongs,
like Anglo-Saxon or Icelandic. Individual words are often
clearly related to other Germanic languages in an interesting but
curiously indiscriminate manner; and on the whole to Icelandic,

148

Gothic, Old Norse or Old German rather than to Swedish. There are even words to which the nearest equivalent is in English—*slaita*, for example, means *sleet*.

FOLKLORE

The *Gutasaga* is the most important story of Gotland, and has been mentioned earlier as a credible historical source. It is perhaps too easy for literate Westerners to underestimate the validity of oral traditions of the sort incorporated in the Saga when it finally came to be written. There are many such examples from remote and self-contained communities, where a kernel of truth is hidden in an elaborate husk of fiction. Thus we find mysterious ancient remains—the ship-graves, the foundations of the Iron Age houses—connected in the Saga with specific pseudo-historical people with surprising accuracy in the light of recent archaeological evidence.

A second type of story is frankly an invention to explain some object or event. The legend of the Old Man of Hoburg (*Hoburgsgubben*) is a case in point. At Hoburg stands a crag looking from certain angles like an enormous head, and below it in the cliff are caves. Hence the crag has been named the Old Man, the caves have been designated his dwelling, and a history of his contact with humans (in which, as usual, great guile is shown by both sides) has been built up. He has been given a wife, another great human-headed crag in the north near Lickershamn, though that crag is also known as 'The Maiden'.

The most famous tale of the Old Man of Hoburg recounts how a peasant nearby, knowing of the wealth in the Old Man's 'Treasure House' (a cave still visible), manoeuvred him, despite the fact that, as a troll, the Old Man was a heathen, into becoming an honorary godfather to the peasant's baby and in that capacity giving the child great wealth. Among various stock mythological tricks the peasant's most successful stratagem was to appeal to the Old Man's pride. A typical Gotlander, the Old

Man was 'not going to be worsted'; so when the peasant listed the wholly imaginary rich presents of successive and equally imaginary other godfathers (including the apostles), the Old Man insisted on outbidding them all. The peasant and his wife staggered away laden with treasure, and they all lived rich and happy ever after. (It may be worth noting that ships carrying treasure and coins have been wrecked on the notorious 'Red Wolf' reef off Hoburg Point, and valuables and specie have sometimes been found on the shore though these wrecks occurred much later than the original legend.)

Other fables are connected with the fact that the oak tree was sacred to Thor, as it usually was to the ruler of the gods in other European religions. Its sacredness was exemplified by the frequency with which it was struck by lightning, compared with other trees, and the lightning was under Thor's control. Near Othem at Othemars farm was a mighty oak which the farmer's wife could see as she sat sewing in her porch. Luckily she had put the scissors open on the threshold while she sewed. Suddenly a great storm blew up and an old crone came running to ask for shelter. The kindness of the farmer's wife was changed to fear when the hag stopped at the threshold glaring at the scissors, which were, of course, in the form of a cross. The woman realised in a flash that this creature must be the dreaded Torspjäku (the Witch of Thor), so, with great presence of mind, made the sign of the cross. The hag shrank back and rushed to the oak, which was immediately hit by lightning, whereupon the witch disappeared. This is obviously an ancient tale from the days when Christianity was asserting its predominance over paganism.

Another story of a witch concerns the Danish invasion of Gotland in 1361. Tradition has it that the leader of this expedition, King Valdemar, had himself spied out the land the previous year. In this task he had been helped by a local witch on condition that he gave her half his expected booty. After his victory he sailed away loaded with loot, never giving a thought to his promise; and in revenge she raised the storm that sank his treasure ship off the Charles Islands.

During this same spying expedition Valdemar is also said to have fallen in love with a farmer's daughter, who helped him and whose house, by the use of a prearranged signal, was left unpillaged by the marauding Danes the following year. This coming to the notice of the Gotlanders, they seized the girl and immured her alive in the tower of Visby's walls now known as 'The Maiden's Tower'. These two stories about Valdemar may be taken as reflecting the contemporary belief that his invasion was somehow facilitated by help given him by some local woman. She may indeed have been walled up alive, perhaps even on the site of 'The Maiden's Tower'; but she could not have been immured in it, as it was not then built.

The motif of a woman influencing Valdemar is again found in a story about a wealthy overweening goldsmith called Nils Guldsmed (which rather suspiciously simply means goldsmith) who went to Valdemar's Danish court in the hope of finding there a man who, unlike the men of Visby, would in his estimation be a worthy husband for his daughter. Aiming high, he obtained an audience of the king himself by telling exaggerated and enticing tales of the riches of Gotland. Later additions have it that Guldsmed told the king of 'the swine eating from silver troughs and the women spinning with golden distaffs'. Whatever the truth of this approach to the Danes, the goldsmith and his daughter later became the theme of many hostile stories.

A folk heroine appears in the story of the Trojeborg maze. One tradition is that the stone rings were built in the Middle Ages by the daughter of an Italian living in Visby. This man, who was very rich but had no obvious source of income, was in fact a very successful pirate. Eventually caught red-handed, he was sentenced to death; but his daughter obtained his pardon by promising the Council of Visby that she would build such a marvellous construction that people would come to see it from far and wide, to the greater glory of the city. What she made was

151

the stone maze of Trojeborg. This tradition at least supports its medieval and probably foreign origin.

Many other tales are local variations of widespread themes: the story of the mermaid married to a mortal; the doings of the 'wee folk', notably 'Bysen', the spirit of the woods, and water-sprites; various quasi-religious cautionary stories with stock villains, like that of the devil and the bailiff, or the man who broke his oath having his cattle turned to stone (an aetiological explanation of the standing stones at Bro); or tales of stock heroes like the Vicar of Bro, who tricked the goblins into giving him the famous golden chalice and then placed it in the church where they could not go. Incidentally, one of the chief Gotlandic goblins is called 'Puck' ('Pukke'). There are also ancient rhymes addressed to recalcitrant windmills, or bellows or other equipment, originally no doubt some sort of simple spell to bring good fortune to the work, but subsequently just an accompaniment to the task—rather like the song the Seven Dwarfs sing while at work in Disney's *Snow White*.

FOOD

Old customs survive in weakened forms but are rapidly disappearing on Gotland, as they did earlier on the Swedish mainland. The Gotlanders have a great tradition of hospitality, and country weddings until recently were celebrated by three whole days of eating and drinking. Some of the ritual on such occasions and also at Christmas was very old. It is an accepted custom in the country to refuse an invitation the first time it is made, and it is good manners to sample a little of every dish.

As regards food Gotlandic specialities are smoked flounder and several mutton dishes, of which the most famous is 'mutton bone broth'. In earlier times, when the diet depended more closely on local produce and there were fewer inhibitions than today about using all parts of the animal, sheep's feet were stewed and served in the broth, one per person. Sheep's heads and calves' heads were a common dish, as in other farming communities before they became too nice. Gotlandic pasties were famous. They were made of black bread and filled with minced pork or fish. As Christmas fare they were stuffed with lard. A variant of this was a great loaf 14in or more in diameter filled with layers of fish and pork and eaten with jacket potatoes. Similar dishes are found in Estonia, and the Gotlandic name for the big loaf was in fact an Estonian word.

In the old days, indeed until the last generation or so and not only in Gotland, it was difficult in Northern Europe to get fresh fruit and green vegetables at the end of winter, and the people ate many wild plants that are now seen only on the plates of cranks or *cognoscenti*. To the Gotlanders the most important were sea-kale (*crambe maritima*), the ancestor of the cultivated vegetable kale; and the sand leek (*allium scorodoprasum*), the shoots of which appear early in the season and were eaten as we eat spring onions, and also made into a soup. In some places, mainly in the south, sea-kale was cultivated and the boundary walls of such 'cabbage plots' can occasionally be traced.

APPENDIX A

SOME NOTABLE CHURCHES

Listed from north to south. See Historical map on p 75

Bunge

Unusually large for North Gotland. Late thirteenth-century Gothic joined to defended tower of about 1200. Good south porch. Unusual murals from turn of thirteenth century in eastern style with greens and browns. Limestone poor-box from mid-thirteenth century in chancel. Impressive eighteenth-century organ originally in Stockholm.

Stenkyrka

On site of one of first stone churches on Gotland. Present church is mid-thirteenth century, with imposing galleried steeple (180ft high) a little later. Good murals from thirteenth and fourteenth centuries inside, including early abstract designs. Elegant pews painted in seventeenth and eighteenth centuries (Wise Virgins early eighteenth century, small landscapes on pew doors 1783–4). Twelfth-century font by 'Maiestatis'. Grave of Licnatus in chancel floor is oldest on Gotland. Stained glass is modern. Near church is good example of country vicarage.

Martebo

A rather unbalanced building, victim of the fourteenth-century recession. Early fourteenth-century Gothic chancel and nave almost as high as Romanesque tower, which was never superseded. Three Gothic doors (as well as a Romanesque one in tower) have particularly good carvings by 'Egypticus'. Painted pulpit (c 1550) one of earliest on Gotland.

Tingstäde

Impressive example of Gotlandic Gothic on commanding site with 180ft steeple. Built from late twelfth to early fourteenth centuries to replace a smaller Romanesque church, it has good Romanesque doors. Nave has fine columns with unusual motifs on capitals. Crucifix early fourteenth century; pulpit, pews, altar late seventeenth and early eighteenth. Good example of traditional entrance to vicarage garden nearby.

Bro

Insignificant, but interesting. Mainly thirteenth-century structure (tower, 1196, is earliest part) on old site. Frieze by Sigraf from earlier church on south front. Early Gothic arch with Romanesque motifs at chancel entrance. Romanesque round west door and windows in tower. Good murals inside from four main periods and elegant eighteenth-century painted pews. Font by Sigraf. Once reputed to own a piece of the True Cross, the church was for centuries a place of pilgrimage and the object of votive prayers. See fine model of eighteenth-century ship as thank-offering. Early crucifix.

Visby Cathedral (St Mary's)

Biggest church on Gotland. Consecrated in 1225. As 'factory' church of German Guild has a great attic storeroom above nave. (Note boom on north front for hoist to attic.) Towers originally had spires, replaced after fire in eighteenth century by present Baroque cupolas. Swerting Chapel, a High Gothic extension of south porch, added mid-fourteenth century, as were Gothic windows in nave. Heavily restored 1899–1901 by A. H. Haig, who replaced much of original ornament. Red sandstone font is thirteenth century and original. Walnut pulpit donated 1684, walnut pews 1945. Some good memorial tablets from sixteenth century.

Hejdeby

A small church with colourful rococo interior. Chancel and nave Romanesque (c 1200), later tower mainly Gothic. Frescoes from late thirteenth to eighteenth centuries, the most recent being particularly gay and complemented by painted pews and ornate pulpit. Fine painted Baroque reredos (1745).

Källunge

An unbalanced church strikingly illustrating how disasters of fourteenth century checked building. Pointed Romanesque tower and small nave (early twelfth century) were never replaced and are now merely appendages to larger later chancel. Very lively carvings on capitals of nave entrance showing famous scene of musicians. Chancel door is excellent example of Gotlandic Gothic. Early Russo-Byzantine fresco in nave, and copy in chancel of Viking bronze burgee (c 1050). Fine painted triptych behind altar (early sixteenth-century German work originally in Visby Cathedral). Font by 'Byzantios'.

Gothem

One of Gotland's biggest churches with a mighty steeple by 'Egypticus' (mid-fourteenth century). Nave has unique frescoes by a German artist (c 1300) showing scenes from Life of Christ with abstract patterns and lively figures—knights, centaurs, dragons and so on. Eighteenth-century wood font. Medieval choir-stalls. Defensive wall round churchyard.

Ekeby

A rather stumpy late thirteenth-century church with colourful interior. Good capitals with abstract floral motifs on both south doors. Thirteenth-century frescoes of apostles in nave with much work by 'The Master of the Passion' set off by eighteenth-century decorative friezes. Late twelfth-century crucifix and font.

Dalhem

One of the biggest and best examples of a Gotlandic Gothic church. Chancel and nave (86ft high and tallest outside Visby) mid-thirteenth century. Steeple (by 'Egypticus') early fourteenth. Unusual carvings on capitals of main porch. Stained glass in north, middle east and south-east windows is earliest on Gotland. Rest of glass is modern, as are murals, to designs of A. H. Haig at turn of century. Fine choir-stalls mainly from fourteenth century.

Eskelhem

A small but interesting church with evidence of earlier buildings, notably in nave and Romanesque features (round-arched door) of tower. Unusual abstract frescoes in nave from mid-thirteenth century, and Church Calendar with Feast Days in runes and Latin and Signs of Zodiac at west end. Early crucifix. Font by 'Byzantios'.

Lojsta

Well proportioned mid-thirteenth-century church with later tower. Excellent mid-thirteenth-century stained glass. Geometrical and decorative murals of same date and more usual fourteenth-century scenes including the Passion and St George and the Dragon. Good fourteenth-century reredos (repainted). Early crucifix.

Stånga

Remarkable south porch and adjacent sculptures, probably the last work of 'Egypticus' and done for a much larger church which the sudden slump ruled out. Fine steeple in 'Egypticus's' more usual style. Big nave with grotesque corbels. Romanesque apsidal chancel. Good thirteenth-century crucifix. Painted sandstone altar-piece from early eighteenth century, as is pulpit. Note iron bar let into wall near porch: this is official 'Gotland ell' (56cm) used of old as against 'Swedish ell' (60cm).

Lye

Has more medieval stained glass than any other church in Scandinavia, also fine carvings (by 'Egypticus') on chancel porch, some good frescoes (including a unique work of Dives and Lazarus by mid-sixteenth-century Danish artist) and splendid late fifteenth-century triptych. High chancel is latest construction (mid-fourteenth century). Nave twelfth century. Tower has curious wooden top. Early stone reliquary carved by Sigraf near west door.

Öja

Splendid example of Gotlandic Gothic, housing great 'Öja crucifix', a masterpiece of late thirteenth-century wooden sculpture. Fine steeple by 'Egypticus'. Church built in stages from early thirteenth (chancel) to mid-fourteenth (steeple) centuries. Very good main porch and interesting carvings on north porch. Simple elegant interior with good frescoes, including unique work by 'Albertus Pictor' from Central Sweden (c 1480). Finely carved stone furnishings (of sandstone from nearby Burgsvik).

CHRONOLOGY OF IMPORTANT EVENTS

400 million years ago	Gotland 10° north of equator in warm tropical seas. Silurian limestone deposits which give island its special character laid down
c 11000 BC	End of latest Ice Age
c 11000–3000 BC	Marked fluctuations in level of water around Gotland produced raised beaches and marine stacks (*raukar*), Ancylus Sea (45m above present level) c 7000 BC and Litorina Sea (20m above present level) c 5000 BC representing biggest changes, which determined areas of first human habitation
c 8000 BC	Date of earliest vegetation so far found on Gotland (a piece of a pine tree)
c 5000 BC	Stone Age man first settled on Gotland
c 1500–c 500 BC	Bronze Age, marked by ship-graves, complex burial cairns and a rich culture. A period of unusually good weather
c 500 BC–c AD 500	Iron Age, ushered in by a marked deterioration in climate. Latter half of period very prosperous from trade with Roman Empire
c 400	First picture-stones
c 500	Sudden collapse of Iron Age culture with collapse of Roman Empire and onset of raids and movements of peoples. Torsburgen and other forts built

c 800– c 1050	Viking Age with distinctive culture and renewed prosperity, orientated to Eastern Europe, Byzantium and Arabia
1029	Conversion of Gotland to Christianity by Norwegian saint and king, Olaf Haraldsson
1161	Treaty of Artlenburg between Gotlanders and Duke Henry of Saxony provides reciprocal trading rights and gives Germans a foothold on Gotland
1164	Consecration of Cistercian monastery at Roma
1288	Civil war between Burghers of Visby and Gotlanders brings in Swedish King Magnus Ladulås, as arbitrator and revives Sweden's interest in Gotland's affairs
1313	Swedish force under King Birger Magnusson defeated by Gotlanders at Röcklingbacke, near Lärbro
1361	Danish King Valdemar Atterdag conquers Gotland, annihilating peasant levies and exacting tribute from Visby
1394–8	Gotland the base of freebooting Vitalian Brothers
1398–1408	Gotland under exemplary rule of Teutonic Order
1408	Eric of Pomerania bases himself on Gotland
1411	Building of Visborg Castle started
1449	Eric of Pomerania expelled. First Danish governor installed
1525	Lübeckers sack Visby, most of the city's churches except the present cathedral being destroyed or damaged
1566	'The Great Shipwreck' off Visby, from 6,000 to 8,000 lives being lost in biggest sea disaster ever known in the Baltic
1570	Under Treaty of Stettin Sweden renounces her claim to Gotland
1645	Under Treaty of Bromsebro Gotland returns to Sweden and becomes a Royal Domain

1676–9	Danes reoccupy Gotland but finally cede it to Sweden under Treaty of Lund, blowing up Visborg Castle before leaving
1741	Linnaeus (Carl von Linné) visits Gotland and produces the first objective account of the island
1791	Gotland's Agricultural Economy Society founded (first in Sweden)
1806	Swedish king offers island to Knights of Malta (recently expelled from Malta by Napoleon), but offer is rejected
1808	Bloodless occupation of Gotland by Russians under Admiral Bodisko for 23 days
1810	Royal decree preserves ruins of Visby (first such decree)
1811	Gotland's Militia established (first in Sweden). First Gotlandic newspaper, *Wisby Tidning*, published
1814	The DBW Philanthropic Society founded in Visby
1829	First steamship visits Visby—SS *Ellida* built in Stockholm
c 1840	Large-scale draining of 'meres' started with introduction of new farming methods
1854–5	Anglo-French fleet in Fårösund to contain Russian Baltic Fleet
1855	Visby Botanic Gardens laid out by DBW Club
1856	First circular steam-saw in operation. Important timber trade with Britain and Germany begins
1865	Gotland's Steamship Company founded
1878	First railway inaugurated on Gotland (from Visby to Hemse). First find of Roman coins
1880	Telephones introduced. Karlsö Wildlife Preservation Society founded
1887	Important excavation of Stone Age sites on Stora Karlsö
1894	Sugar-beet factory opened at Roma

K

GOTLAND

1904	First electricity generating station started. Gotland's first industrial exhibition
1905	First motor car on Gotland (2½hp German Dürrkop)
1906	First motor-bus service started
1908	Bunge Folk Museum opened
1911	First lifesaving station set up near Hoburgen
1915	German minelaying cruiser *Albatross* driven ashore by Russian warships on west coast
1918	Telephone system connected to mainland
1933	First regular passenger air service started to Stockholm (with flying boats from Tingstäde Lake)
1944	SS *Hansa* ferry sunk by mine with loss of ninety lives. Regular airmail service introduced
1954	Undersea electric power connection made to mainland Sweden using sea bed as return transmission path (first in world)
1960	Railway services terminated

BIBLIOGRAPHY

THERE are very few books or even feature articles in English on Gotland. Most are unobtainable outside specialised libraries. Many of the excellent Swedish publications on the island have a summary in English. The main works used by the author are listed below.

BOBERG, FERDINAND. *Visby*. Watercolours by F. Boberg, text by Erik Lundberg (Stockholm, 1939)

Boken om Gotland, 2 vols (Stockholm, 1945). A survey by various authors to commemorate 300 years of Swedish rule over Gotland

DU CHAILLU, PAUL. *Land of the Midnight Sun*, 2 vols (1881). Vol I, Chapter XXVII, covers Gotland

EDQUIST, DAGMAR, and PETERSENS, LENNART AF. *Gotland: Treasure Island of the Baltic* (Stockholm, 1960)

GRAVES, S. R. *A Yachting Cruise in the Baltic* (1863). Chapter VI deals with Gotland

HANSSON, HANS HARALD. *Gotlands Bronsålder* (Stockholm, 1927)

HEALES, ALFRED. *The Churches of Gotland (other than those of Wisby)* (1888). A very limited private edition

——. *The Ecclesiology of Gotland* (1889)

JAKOBSON, HENNING. *Gotland—Landet Annorlunda* (Visby, 1966)

JANSE, OTTO. *Visby Stadsmur* (Uppsala, 1962)

LAGERLÖF, E. and SVAHNSTRÖM, G. *Gotlands Kyrkor* (Stockholm, 1966)

LEMKE, UWE. *Gotland. Ein Geistergeschichtlicher Quellort* (Stuttgart, 1970). Mainly architectural with nothing after 1550

LINDBLOM, A. and SVAHNSTRÖM, G. *Gotländska Stenmästare* (Malmö, 1959)

LINDQUIST, SUNE. *Gotlands Bildsteine*, 2 vols (Stockholm, 1941)

LINNÉ, CARL VON. *Gotländska Resa 1741* (Stockholm, 1969). Linnaeus' famous visit to the island with notes by Knut Hagberg

GOTLAND

GOTLAND

GOTLAND

GOTLAND

GOTLAND

GOTLAND

LITHBERG, NILS. *Gotlands Stenålder* (Stockholm, 1914)

LUNDBERG, ERIK. *Visby: Kyrkoruinerna och Domkyrkan* (Stockholm, 1962)

——. *Visby*. Watercolours by F. Boberg, text by Erik Lundberg (Stockholm, 1939)

NYLÉN, ERIK. *Die Jüngere Vorrömische Eizenseit Gotlands* (Uppsala, 1955)

——. *An Isle of Sagas: Legends and Folklore from Gotland* (Visby, 1931)

PETTERSSON, BENGT. *Gotlands Orkidéer* (Stockholm, 1951). English summary. Lovely photographs

ROOSVAL, JOHNNY. *Die Kirchen Gotlands* (Stockholm, 1911)

——. *Die Steinmeister Gotlands* (Stockholm, 1918)

——. *Den Gotländska Ciceronen* (Stockholm, 1926)

——. *Gotländska Vitrarius* (Stockholm, 1950). Beautiful illustrations of medieval stained glass

——. *Gotlands Kyrkokonst* (Stockholm, 1952)

SANSOM, WILLIAM. 'Riches of Gotland', *The Geographical Magazine* (August, 1962)

SJÖBERG, ÅKE (ed). *Historia Kring Gotland* (Stockholm, 1963). Useful essays by experts on various aspects of Gotland's history

SÖDERBERG, BENGT G. *Gotland i Historien* (Visby, 1968)

——. *Götlandska Kalkmålingar* (Visby, 1971)

——. *Vad skall jag se på Gotland?* (Stockholm, 1966). An excellent little guidebook in the Swedish Tourist Association's series

——. *Visby—En Vandring Genom Sekler* (Visby, 1973)

STENBERGER, MÅRTEN. *Das Grabfeld von Västerbjers auf Gotland* (Lund, 1943)

——. *Vallhagar: a Migration Period Settlement on Gotland/Sweden*, 2 vols (Copenhagen, 1955)

THORDEMAN, BENGT. *Korsbetningen* (Lund, 1964). An account of the excavation of the mass graves of the peasant soldiers killed outside Visby in 1361. English summary

Visby och Gotland i Bilder. Visby and Gotland in Pictures (Visby, 1970). Annotated captions in Swedish, English, German and Finnish to a good selection of colour photographs

Visby and Its Historic Sights with a Brief Survey of Gotland's and Visby's Past. An informative short guidebook

WÅHLIN, HANS. *Visby and the Ancient Civilisation of Gotland* (Stockholm, 1938)

YARHAM, E. P. 'The Baltic's Tale of Ancient Glory', *The American-Scandinavian Review*, vol XLVI, No 2 (June, 1958)

ZETTERLING, A. *Bulverket i Tingstäde Träsk* (Stockholm, 1935)

BIBLIOGRAPHY

There is considerable incidental information on various aspects of Gotland in general works such as:

ANDERSON, INGVAR. *History of Sweden* (1965)
BLUNT, WILFRED. *The Complete Naturalist. A Life of Linnaeus* (1970). Contains a summary of Linnaeus' visit to Gotland
FOOTE, P. G., and WILSON, D. M. *The Viking Achievement* (1970)
JONES, GWYN. *History of the Vikings* (1968)
LUNDBERG, ERIK. *Byggnadskonsten i Sverige under Medeltiden 1000–1400* (Stockholm, 1940)
Medieval Wooden Sculpture in Sweden, by various experts, 5 vols (Uppsala/Stockholm, 1964)

There is more specialised information on Gotland in various learned journals. Most important is the annual survey of historical and cultural research on and concerning the island, *Gotländskt Arkiv*, published each year (with an English summary) since 1929 by Föreningen Gotlands Fornvänner in Visby. The annual publication of the Royal Academy of History, Letters and Antiquities in Stockholm, *Fornvännen*, also deals with Gotlandic matters from time to time.

On Gotland itself handbooks to museums and notes on various churches and other sites of interest are often available in English.

While this book was in preparation, the following articles on Gotland appeared in English-language periodicals:

CERUTTI, JAMES. 'Gotland, Sweden's Treasure Island', *National Geographic Magazine*, vol 144, No 2 (August, 1973)
GASKELL, GORDON. 'Sweden's Golden Island', *Reader's Digest* (October, 1973)
SPENCER, ARTHUR. 'Gotland's Unknown Churches', *Country Life* vol CLIV, No 3989 (6 December, 1973)

ACKNOWLEDGEMENTS

O F the many persons who have given me help and encouragement in the compilation of this book I should like particularly to thank Dr and Mrs Gunnar Svahnström, of Gotlands Fornsal, and Hr Agne Jonasson, of Gotlands Turist Förening. I am also indebted to Professors Foote and Wilson of the Department of Scandinavian Studies of University College, London, Joseph Crabtree and the Librarian of the Department.

The Swedish Institute, the Swedish Tourist Traffic Association and the Royal Library in Stockholm have also generously allowed me to use their ample resources.

Finally I would like to pay tribute to my wife's help in many ways, not least in typing most of the manuscript.

INDEX

Page numbers in italics indicate illustrations

Martebo, 123, 154
Masons, *see* Architects
'Master Jeweller of Broa', 155
'Master of Lye', glass-painter, 131
'Master of the Passion', painter, *54*, 131, 134, 156
Mästerby, 134
Mästermyr, 56
Maypoles, 141
Mecklenberg, 70
Meres, 19, 22, 28, 84, 94, 161
'Mill Tower' (*Kvarntornet*), 116
Minever, 61
Mink, 87
Motor cars, 106, 139, 161
Mulberries, 113, 120
Munthe, Prof Henrik, 21
Murals, *see* Wall paintings
Museums, 141–2; *see also* Bottarve, Bunge, Gotlands Fornsal, Kovik, *Lojstahallen*
Muscicapa albicolla, 34
Mutton, 86, 152
Mycenae, 41

Napier, Admiral Sir Charles, 81
Napoleon, 79
När, 131
National Assembly, 59, 64
National Parks, 26
Nature reserves, 26
Neopilina, 16
Nevasa, 104
Newspapers, *see* Press
Norrby, Sören, 73
Norrköping, 100, 105
Norrlanda, 130
Novgorod, 61, 66, 132
Norway, 14, 43, 55, 56, 57, 81, 92, 124
Nydquist & Holm, 111
Nynäshamn, 104, 196

Öja, *54*, 95, 130, 134, 135, 158
Olaf Haraldsson, King, 58

Öland, 11, 67, 74, 104, 106
'Old Apothecary's Shop' (*Gamla Apoteket*), *18*, *109*, 118
'Old Man of Hoburg' (*Hoburgsgubben*), 19, 149–50
Orchids, 23, 31
Ordovician Age, 14
Oscar I, King, 111
Oseberg ship, 56
Oskarshamn, 104
Östergarnsholm, 105
Owen, Samuel, 96

Packhusplan, 118
Palaeophonus, 16
Paris, 61
Pärk, game, 140
Peat, 94
Pet, 82
Petrus de Dacia, *126*, 141, 146
Pews, 129, 154, 156
Picture-stones, 46–7, 56–9, *89*, 109
Pilina, 16
Pinguicula alpina, 31
Pitprops, 87
Planks, 88
Plants, 30–2
Poland, 14
Polhen, 96
Polhem, Cristoffer, 105, 146
Politics, 99
Pomerania, 70
Population, 61, 98, 102
Porcacci, Tomasso, 63
Porches, *53*, 123, 127, 128, 154–8
Ports, 77, 78–9, 105
Post-Gothic style, 134–5
Posts, 106–7, 117, 162
Potatoes, 78
'Powder Tower' (*Kruttornet*), 115, 145
Power, 93–5, 146
Press, 83, 110, 148
Publishing, 110
Pulpits, 129, 155, 156